W9-BYZ-629

Japanese-Style Gardens

Brian Funk and Sarah Schmidt
Editors

BROOKLYN
BOTANIC
GARDEN

Elizabeth Peters
EXECUTIVE EDITOR

Sarah Schmidt
MANAGING EDITOR

Anthony S. Aiello
SCIENCE EDITOR

Joni Blackburn
COPY EDITOR

Manny Jose
ART DIRECTOR

Scot Medbury
PRESIDENT

Elizabeth Scholtz
DIRECTOR EMERITUS

Handbook #201

Copyright © 2015 by Brooklyn Botanic Garden, Inc.

ISBN 978-1-889538-91-4

Printed in China by Ocean Graphic International

♻ Printed with soy-based inks on
postconsumer recycled paper.

Guides for a Greener Planet are published by
Brooklyn Botanic Garden, 1000 Washington Avenue,
Brooklyn, NY 11225.

Learn more at bbg.org/handbooks.

Cover: The Japanese Hill-and-Pond Garden at Brooklyn Botanic Garden in early autumn.
Above: Brooklyn Botanic Garden's Shinto shrine beneath a blanket of snow.

Japanese-Style Gardens

What Do We Mean by Japanese Garden?

Brian Funk

As curator of the Japanese Hill-and-Pond Garden at Brooklyn Botanic Garden, for 16 years I have had the responsibility and privilege of working in a beautiful naturalistic refuge in the midst of a huge urban environment. As an escape from the city, this Japanese-inspired garden has long been popular not just with tourists but with New Yorkers too. If you sit in the viewing pavilion over the pond, you will hear the sounds of wind blowing and of water falling, smell the fragrance of flowers, and see a harmonious landscape filled with beautiful plants as well as wildlife like turtles, ducks, and koi. Enclosed by a traditional Japanese roofed fence and entered through weathered wooden gates, this garden allows you to leave the city behind and enter a more elemental environment.

Our garden is one of the oldest public Japanese gardens in the United States, but it is still evolving—no garden is ever truly finished. Those that have survived this long have usually gone through many transitions, some of which may have been controversial. As I care for this one—pruning, weeding, cleaning, performing repairs, and making improvements to fit my vision of a Japanese garden—I always aim to maintain the garden's integrity. In doing so, I often return to the question of what, in essence, it means to have a "Japanese" garden outside of Japan.

When Takeo Shiota designed and built this garden in 1914, he was embarking on something of an experiment. A novice designer at the time, he was asked to create a garden in a style unfamiliar to most people, in a chaotic and crowded city, with limited funds and a lack of quality materials. Pulling off this project was a remarkable feat. When it opened the following year, the garden probably seemed a little bit crude and unfinished, but it soon became a celebrated and well-respected example of the Japanese style in America.

Shiota did not try to re-create a traditional garden from his homeland; rather, I believe, he aimed to please his Western audience with a landscape that provided a postcard scene of Japan. He interpreted garden and architectural styles liberally, including in his plan, for example, a viewing pavilion built in the style of a teahouse.

Takeo Shiota created a rolling landscape for BBG's Japanese Hill-and-Pond Garden that highlights the beauty of the changing seasons.

His unusual choice of installing a Shinto shrine and torii, along with two five-foot bronze cranes on the shore of the island (since removed), made for particularly exotic vistas. His greatest achievement may have been the way he established the basic contours of the landscape—dredging the existing pond and using the soil to create artificial hills—but his single most successful element was the waterfall, designed and constructed using local Manhattan schist. Not only does it make for a beautiful scene, but its lovely sound also has the effect of insulating the spot from the city beyond.

Japanese Gardens in the United States

Interest in Japanese gardening outside of Japan had begun to grow just before the turn of the 19th century, after Japan opened its borders following centuries of shogunate military rule and isolationism. The new Meiji emperor made a tremendous effort to share Japanese culture and art with the world. At several world's fairs and expositions, Japan installed pavilions, gardens, and houses. Europeans and Americans became enamored with Japan's superb artistic traditions. Japanism became chic, and many wealthy people commissioned Japanese gardens of their own to be built on their estates.

Public gardens, with Brooklyn Botanic Garden leading the way, began installing Japanese gardens to showcase what was becoming recognized as one the finest garden forms in the world. But by the beginning of World War II, they started falling out of favor, and anti-Japanese sentiment and vandalism resulted in the closure of most public ones, including ours. After the war, though, interest slowly returned. Many existing public Japanese gardens, like that of the Huntington, were restored, and new ones, like the Portland Japanese Garden, were built across the country.

At the same time, homeowners began to try Japanese gardening, with mixed results. Good information, qualified designers and builders, and quality materials were hard to find for many years. I remember visiting garden shows in the 1970s and '80s and seeing tacky designs that included round plastic pools, dwarf weeping cherry trees, miniature bridges, and white marble chips as groundcover. Such attempts misrepresented Japanese gardens to many Westerners, even professionals. When I was starting out in my career as a horticulturist and landscape designer, I didn't really understand the concept myself. Many of the supposed Japanese gardens I'd seen were odd, tasteless, uninspiring—or all these things.

At that time, I worked mostly with native plants in a naturalistic style influenced by Jens Jensen and the prairie style. But I had always had an interest in Japanese culture and had worked with bonsai. This eventually led me to reconsider Japanese gardening, which is another way to express the natural world on a smaller scale. When I went to Japan in 2000, I became a true believer. The beauty of the gardens there is awe inspiring, and I found a much higher level of art to aspire to. The modest stroll garden at Murinan in Kyoto probably influenced me the most. There

The Japanese Hill-and-Pond Garden in 1916, not long after it opened. The waterfall was created using local stone and remains one of the garden's most pleasing elements.

are grander gardens in Japan, but this simple one, about the size of a large American backyard, represented something that was within the realm of possibility.

Since then, appreciation for and knowledge of authentic Japanese gardens in the United States has grown. Qualified designers and builders are now easier to research and find online, and publications like *Sukiya Living* provide excellent resources and education for home gardeners and professionals. Japanese sister cities also continue to work with their corresponding North American cities to create new or better gardens, and many impressive public gardens have been built here in recent decades.

Japanese-style gardens in North America will never be quite the same as true Japanese gardens, but I believe that it's possible to capture some of the essence of this centuries-old tradition. A collection of lanterns, bridges, and pagodas does not make a garden authentic. Instead, a good garden in the Japanese tradition should be a carefully designed environment where the natural world is distilled in a way that fosters an intimate connection. Patterns and rhythms found in nature are expressed in a sort of three-dimensional landscape painting. Spending time in this space feels nurturing in a way that promotes reflection. The best Japanese-inspired gardens are able to achieve this regardless of location, and this is what I strive for as curator of Brooklyn Botanic Garden's Japanese Hill-and-Pond Garden. As you read about and visit as many of these gardens as you can, you will gain a deeper understanding of this wonderful tradition.

Japanese Gardens in the Modern World

Hoichi Kurisu

I was born in 1939 in a small rice-farming village an hour north of the city of Hiroshima, Japan. At that time, the world was in turmoil. The Second World War had begun, and Japan was experiencing material shortages of just about everything, including food. But as children we had no awareness of these things. We grew up playing in nature. We had no commercially manufactured toys. Instead, we explored the surrounding forests and valleys.

We delighted in foraging for food—mushrooms, fiddlehead ferns, chestnuts—and there was a wild pear tree at the base of a mountain. We would throw rocks to chase away the monkeys that sat in it so we could pick the pears. We made slingshots and bamboo traps to catch fish in the streams. We also helped in the rice fields. When it was time to plant and later to harvest the rice, the whole village worked together.

I remember one early spring day when I was about three years old, while playing in my grandfather's garden, I discovered the small, vibrant red shoots of a peony just emerging from the earth. I was fascinated! I will never forget this feeling of pure excitement. Later, I even took my grandfather's spade and tried to transplant these peonies, which just got me into a lot of trouble.

This carefree, village childhood came to an abrupt end in 1945, when the United States dropped the atomic bomb on Hiroshima and ended World War II. While a mountain ridge protected my village from the bomb's terrible destruction, its impact changed the course of all Japan. In the aftermath of the war, the rush to modernize, westernize, and industrialize virtually destroyed the traditional family structure I knew as a young child, as well as the social and educational systems. It changed people's minds about almost everything. Instead of going to high school, nearly all my classmates left the village to work in factories. Japan's culture became much more money driven, and Western countries were considered the ideal models for growth.

I was fortunate enough to attend university in Tokyo, and when I graduated, the United States was perceived as a dream country. Despite substantial anti-American feelings among some students, many young Japanese people were looking to the

Anderson Japanese Gardens in Rockford, Illinois. Gardens foster a connection to nature that can restore physical, cognitive, and emotional balance in an increasingly urbanized world.

West. In 1962, I bought a plane ticket to Los Angeles and, with no definite purpose in mind, went to see what all the hype was about.

When I arrived, two things happened. First, I spent the first six months being amazed—at what Americans had and what they were spending. There was no comparison in Japanese life to America's post-war affluence—Lincoln Continentals bigger than my apartment in Tokyo, Cadillacs that might as well have been spaceships. The houses were huge too. Even the steaks were huge! There was so much *stuff* everywhere. Second, I joined my father, who was working as a landscaper in the area. In doing so, I instantly rediscovered my childhood passion for plants, soil, and rocks. I knew then that I wanted to work in landscape the rest of my life.

A Rapidly Changing World

At the same time, as we worked in wealthy neighborhoods like Beverly Hills and Santa Monica, I began to sense an imbalance between Americans' material affluence and their quality of life. I saw many lavish homes and gardens but discovered that the owners were often unhappy. Many were going through divorces, or for whatever other reasons, were rarely home. I felt that somehow gardens could address this imbalance.

Japanese aesthetics were popular in mainstream America then, and Japanese gardens had long been a cultural export. In 1960s California, I saw many very strange-looking attempts at Japanese garden design—full of enthusiasm but lacking authenticity—and knew that I could do better. I imagined building gardens like the famous ancient gardens of Kyoto, so after two years in California, I returned to Japan to study with a master.

But I never made it to Kyoto. Instead, I was introduced to Kenzo Ogata, a renowned Tokyo-based landscape designer, and began an apprenticeship with him. On a morning in May, Ogata took me to one of his residential garden projects. I will never forget the feeling of stepping into that garden. Immediately, I was overcome with an indescribable sense of peace, tranquility, and comfort. I thought, *this is it.* It was the same feeling I had experienced during my childhood in wild nature—a total disappearance of boundaries between myself and the natural world—a feeling of fascination and almost unconscious oneness with nature.

The naturalistic style in which Ogata worked was called *zokinoniwa*. This modern style was much different from the traditional Kyoto styles and unlike anything I had seen before. It affected me powerfully, and I wanted with all my heart to learn more about it.

I found that zoki-style gardens took their inspiration from the native landscape beyond the outskirts of Tokyo. Compared with traditional-style gardens, they were much less formal, using deciduous trees and other plants that are sensitive to seasonal changes. Japanese society was changing rapidly at that time, and Ogata was creating gardens to respond to contemporary needs. I believe this is still the most important mission of Japanese gardens today. The techniques of Japanese garden design have not changed much—they are as effective now as they were centuries ago—but the world outside the garden has changed dramatically. As designers striving to make gardens that respond to human needs, it is our duty to consider the world around us.

Look at the global trends today and how they affect all of us. We increasingly interact with and depend on technology in daily life. We are shopping, looking for directions, reading, and listening to music more via our phones and computers and less by interacting with others or with the physical world. Recently, on a layover in Detroit with my crew, we went to a sushi restaurant near our terminal. At the table we discovered a tablet computer. I thought it was a video game, but actually it was the menu!

No waiters took our order—we simply touched the picture of the sushi we desired, and it appeared at our table a few minutes later. Much more convenient than the bamboo fish traps we built in my childhood! Still, I can't help feeling something has been lost along the way. As innovative technologies transform our world with new profit-driven efficiencies, I wonder what the long-term cost of eliminating human interaction will be.

Urbanization is also reducing the time we spend in nature in our daily lives. More than half the world's population lives in cities now, and that proportion is expected to reach two thirds by 2050, according to estimates by the United Nations. And spending more time near other people doesn't necessarily mean more human connection—the dynamics of big cities can often amplify a sense of alienation and loneliness.

Every element in a garden is said to have an inherent force, or _kisei_, that determines the way it may be placed. This force may be expressed vertically or horizontally or in combination.

Stress is also changing us, and it has become so common that most people assume it is inevitable. The World Health Organization has called stress "the health epidemic of the 21st century." The costs of stress are significant: 75 percent of health-care costs are due to chronic illness, and stress is the number one cause of chronic illness. The American Psychological Association reports that stress levels are on the rise not just among adults but also among teens and even grade school children.

What Role Can Gardens Play?

There is a significant and growing body of global research documenting the power of nature to heal us, relax us, and restore physical, cognitive, and emotional balance. Reducing and preventing stress is one of the major ways that gardens affect our well-being. But how, exactly, can Japanese gardens meet contemporary human needs? The oldest known treatise on Japanese garden making, the *Sakuteiki*, discusses the "art of setting stones." At one point, it instructs the reader to "ishi no kowan ni shitagahite," or "follow the request of the stone." Likewise, we can look to nature for direction.

Ogata taught that every item in a garden—plant, tree, rock—expresses an inherent force, or energy, that must be recognized in order to create harmony in the garden. We call this quality *kisei*. Kisei may be expressed vertically or horizontally, or in any combination of the two. Identifying the inherent kisei of each item allows the designer to arrange items in a harmonious way. This is something like the way a conductor would balance the performance of each musician and instrument of an orchestra to produce a symphony.

Kisei applies to individual items, to groups of items, and to a design as a whole. In other words, kisei is scalable. And like the symphony, when the kisei of garden elements is harmonized, something greater than the sum of its parts emerges. In the garden, we call this *ma*. Ma is a very complex concept that permeates almost every aspect of Japanese culture. The word *ma* has no literal translation but can be referred to as "space" or "void." Ma may be expressed temporally, spatially, even socially—and as a combination of any of these.

As linear space, ma could be the length of a tatami mat, or in three dimensions, the space between stones in a dry rock garden. The punctuation of movement and sound amounts to a lot of ma in Noh theater and in traditional Japanese dance. The ma, or empty space, created between elements of ikebana is just as important as the flowers and branches themselves. In Japanese martial arts such as kendo, another type of ma, *ma-ai*, refers to the critical, dynamic distance between two opponents, determined by skill, potential power, and psychological strength. In daily life, ma can exist between two people when they bow to greet each other. There is physical space between two people, but also perceived space, activated by intention and respect.

Japanese gardens have ma that is physical, visual, and temporal. But no matter whether ma is seen, heard, or entered into physically, above all, ma must be *felt*. In

The space between elements can be referred to as *ma*, a complex concept that determines the way gardens and other works of art are experienced.

the garden, ma should be an experience that engages all of our being. When this occurs, we are experiencing a space that cannot be measured—a mental space. This is the Japanese garden. Without this mental space, there is no Japanese garden.

There is a tendency to focus too much on perfecting technique and craftsmanship when making Japanese gardens. We can teach these things, but perfect craftsmanship alone does not make the garden good. I'm not degrading perfection, but somehow what makes people feel true comfort in the garden is beyond any single element.

As the famous kabuki actor Onoe Kikugoro once told a student who had asked him how to be a great performer, "There are two kinds of ma—one that can be taught and one that cannot. After I teach the first kind, you must go on to master the second by yourself." The second kind of ma has to do with ego. Both mastering a craft and becoming receptive to the world around us require humility.

The time-honored techniques of Japanese garden design were developed to direct one's experience in specific ways, to lessen preoccupation with the self and foster an increased awareness of nature and our relation to it. This simple transformation of thought meets a fundamental human need, now more so than ever. When you experience ma in the garden, you feel a sense of connection not only to the nature around you but also on a much larger, even universal scale. This receptivity reminds us of the timeless cycles of change and regeneration that support our world, and of which we are a part.

Important Garden Styles and Their Historical Roots

Marc Peter Keane

The art of gardening has been developing in Japan for 1,500 years, and over that time, various forms and styles have been created in response to changes in society and culture. Gardens that were designed by aristocrats over a thousand years ago are different from those designed for military lords in a later era or by tea masters after that.

Despite these differences, there are certain underlying design principles that all Japanese gardens have in common. First and foremost, these gardens reflect the natural world. Rather than being based on man-made patterns, such as geometric forms, Japanese gardens emulate nature. The layout is asymmetric, pruning reflects natural growth, and a weathered patina of age is appreciated and enhanced rather than prevented through maintenance.

When asked what the most essential quality of the garden is, Japanese gardeners will often answer, *shiki*, the four seasons. Their job, as they see it, is to distill the beauty of the changing seasons by placing plants and other natural features close at hand, in the garden, where they can be appreciated as part of daily life.

Another key quality is a simple palette. The garden is not seen as a repository for nature's bounty or as a collection of exotic wonders. Instead, the designer chooses from among the many possible materials a few to represent the entirety of nature. The peacefulness associated with Japanese gardens is the result of this restrained palette. One of those materials is stone, a fundamental element of Japanese gardens. Typically, this takes the form of weathered boulders. Stones are considered to be the bones of a garden, as seen in the opening line of the *Sakuteiki*, Japan's ancient gardening text, which states that making a garden is the art of setting stones.

A final word about maintenance: To a great extent, the feeling of a Japanese garden comes from the hand of the gardener who cares for it. The graceful shape of a well-pruned pine tree is the most obvious example, but even something as simple as a soft moss groundcover is likely the result of daily sweeping, weeding, and watering. Without necessarily seeing the gardener at work, a visitor senses this care upon entering the garden, and it feels good.

The water's edge at Kenrokuen in Kanazawa. This Edo-period stroll garden was created on the grounds of Kanazawa Castle and is considered one of the greatest gardens in Japan.

The dry stone garden at Ryoanji Temple in Kyoto, Japan, is considered one of the finest extant examples of this historical style. It is intended to be viewed but not entered.

Karesansui: Contemplative Stone Gardens

Karesansui are sculptural, enigmatic gardens that evoke scenes from the natural world through the restrained use of boulders, some plants, and at times, raked gravel. Unlike other gardens, karesansui are intended to be contemplated from an adjacent room rather than physically entered. In Japanese, the word *karesansui* is written with the three characters for dry-mountain-water, in which mountain-water, *sansui*, means landscape, or more broadly, nature. *Kare* refers to the fact that water in the garden is represented symbolically through patterns of stones.

Initially, in the Heian (794–1185) and Kamakura (1185–1333) periods, these stone arrangements were created in large, open garden situations. From the Muromachi period (1333–1568) onward, they became more formalized and were built in walled courtyards adjacent to architecture. Historically, these buildings were the residences of military lords or the abbots' residence halls in Zen temples, but in present-day Japan, karesansui gardens can be found in all manner of locations, including restaurants, hotels, museums, businesses, and private homes.

The classic form of a courtyard karesansui garden includes several groupings of boulders, set upright or prone in a field of white sand, such as those in the garden at Ryoanji Temple, which has been listed as a UNESCO World Heritage Site. The stones are typically set in groups of odd numbers and form arrangements that are loosely triangular in shape. The repetitive lines raked into the sand represent waves, and the stones themselves evoke islands in the sea. There are, however, many other ways to create karesansui gardens. The raked white sand can be replaced by a field of moss. A dry stream or waterfall can be represented instead of the ocean.

In the West, karesansui are often referred to as Zen gardens or meditation gardens, descriptions not used in Japan. It is important to understand that karesansui gardens were not developed by Zen priests as an aid to meditation and are not used as the focal object of seated meditation. A karesansui garden built within a Zen temple might contain allegorical Buddhist imagery, such as that of Sumeru, the central mountain of Buddhist cosmology, but there are many more occasions in which karesansui gardens have been built in secular situations for decorative purposes. In these cases, the gardens are more properly interpreted as three-dimensional, sculptural versions of ink landscape paintings.

Roji: Tea Gardens

During the 16th and 17th centuries, a new cultural practice called *chanoyu*, the tea ceremony, developed in Japan, centered on the drinking of powdered tea. Practitioners of this art would gather in small groups in rustic teahouses to share a simple meal and bowls of whisked tea. In order to enter the teahouse, an entry garden was created that emulated a forest path, so that the guests arriving for a tea gathering would have a chance to settle their minds before entering the teahouse.

The tea garden at the Adachi Museum of Art in Yasugi, Japan, includes the characteristic stepping-stone path that encourages guests to walk slowly as they approach the teahouse.

This pathlike garden was called a *roji*, which originally meant "alleyway" but later was written with different characters that have the meaning "dewy ground," a reference to a Buddhist paradise described in the Lotus Sutra.

The classical urban tea garden is designed in an unassuming way, with nothing showy or ostentatious: no brightly flowering plants, no special ornamental stones, nothing that draws attention to itself or implies wealth and social status. One of the basic tenets of the chanoyu is that it be egalitarian. The plantings consist mostly of evergreen trees and shrubs and a moss groundcover. There are many ways to design a tea garden, but a fully developed one has certain requisite parts. The guest first enters through an outer gate that separates the everyday world from that of the tea gathering to heighten the latter aesthetically and spiritually. After entering the outer gate, guests find a simple path made of stepping-stones that leads them through the garden. The stepping-stone path slows the pace of the guests passing through the garden and makes them more aware of their surroundings.

Next, the guests arrive at a small roofed bench, where they wait for the host to summon them with a silent bow before they move on to the teahouse. The time they spend waiting at the bench allows them to prepare, physically and mentally, for the tea gathering. Once called forward, the guests then pass through a middle gate, a simple structure that divides the garden into outer *roji* and inner *roji* and symbolically expresses passage into the pure world within.

Once inside the middle gate, the guests find an arrangement of low stones called a *tsukubai*, which includes a stone water basin. Each person in turn crouches down and scoops some water from the basin with a wooden ladle to cleanse the mouth and hands before entering the teahouse. Together, the forestlike plantings, elongated path, and various thresholds within the garden evoke the feeling that the guests have left the city and traveled far into the mountains to the seclusion of a hermit's hut.

Kaiyushiki-teien: Stroll Gardens

In the relatively stable social climate of Japan's Edo period (1600–1868), the military lords, or daimyo, began to build large estates near castles in their home provinces to act as both private residences and official reception facilities. Over several generations, these estates grew in size, with large gardens as a central feature. The gardens were traversed by a series of meandering paths that allowed the lord and his guests to enjoy the changing views as they perambulated the garden. For this reason, this type of garden is often referred to as a stroll garden, *kaiyushiki-teien*. During the social upheaval of the Meiji period (1868–1912), the status of the military lords was abolished, and the ancient provinces were reinvented as modern prefectures. Many of these large stroll gardens were either destroyed or turned into public gardens or parks, some of which still exist.

Korakuen is a stroll garden created around 1700 by the lord of Okayama Castle. It was once used to entertain palace guests but is now open to the public.

Historically, there were many variations on the stroll garden, but they generally included certain representative features. The most prominent was the central lake. An irregularly shaped, shallow body of water, the lake gave the garden a sense of breadth and openness. The shoreline might also twist into a series of coves, creating smaller, more intimate spaces. It was sometimes possible to travel around these lakes by small boat, allowing for yet a different view of the garden.

Edo period kaiyushiki-teien also sometimes contained allegorical scenes that the host could reveal to his guests as they strolled through the garden. Chinese icons gleaned from classical stories were popular, such as the arched moon bridge and representations of Mount Wu, known for Buddhist pilgrimages, and Hangzhou's long Su Causeway crossing West Lake. *Meisho*, famous scenic views from around Japan—familiar to visitors from woodblock prints—were also re-created, including Mount Fuji and the pine-covered sandbar at Amanohashidate.

One garden design element often employed in stroll gardens is called borrowed scenery, *shakkei*. This is accomplished by linking a distant view of the landscape in the background with a section of the garden in the foreground to create a single scene through the skillful arrangement of a middle-ground feature such as a wall or hedge. The result is a living painting intended to be seen from a particular point within the garden.

Courtyard gardens were developed by urban artisans and merchants to bring nature into their homes. They are now common in Japanese inns and guesthouses.

Tsuboniwa: Townhouse Courtyard Gardens

The Edo period also saw a great increase in the wealth and cultural development of the merchants and artisans who lived in Japan's large, crowded cities. They began to build more substantial residences that had a narrow frontage and extended deep into the city block. Typically, a workshop or shop building called the *omoteya* faced the street. Farther back was the residence, called the *omoya*, and beyond that was a storehouse called a *kura*. In between were small courtyard openings that let light and air into the buildings. In time, the owners began installing small gardens in the spaces.

These small gardens are called *tsuboniwa*, or sometimes *senzai*. Both terms were originally used for estate gardens of the Heian period. Their adoption by the townsfolk of the Edo period was a lighthearted attempt to emulate the culture of the ancient great families described in *The Tale of Genji* and other classic stories of days gone by.

The designs of tsuboniwa, which are still popular in Japan, incorporate many elements of tea gardens, such as lanterns, stepping-stones, water basins, moss groundcover, and subdued plantings of evergreen shrubs and small trees. What makes these gardens remarkable is the way they bring the essence of the natural world into the middle of the crowded, densely built city. They may be no more than the size of a few *tatami* mats, and yet they keep the subtleties of the natural world and the changing seasons close at hand in the daily life of the urban middle class.

Important Eras in Japanese Garden Design

Heian period (794–1185)

Heiankyo (now Kyoto) was the cultural and political capital of Japan during this time, and the imperial family and other aristocrats controlled society. Gardens were typically built in the southern courts of multi-dwelling residences and were influenced by such factors as Buddhism and traditional taboos. The classic garden design treatise the *Sakuteiki* was written during this period.

Kamakura period (1185–1333)

The military class gained control over society during this period and made Kamakura the political capital. Garden design was influenced by the introduction of Zen Buddhism from China as well as by arts such as ink landscape painting and miniature tray landscapes. It was during this time that early dry gardens (*karesansui*) emerged.

Muromachi period (1333–1568)

During this period, the Muromachi district of Kyoto became the political capital. In the residences of military lords (daimyo), as well as in Zen Buddhist temples, karesansui evolved to include arrangements of stones placed in walled courtyards. By the end of this period, understated tea gardens (*roji*) developed as the physical and spiritual approach to tea gatherings.

Momoyama period (1568–1600)

The castle at Momoyama was the seat of political power during this brief period, known for its exuberant artistic culture. The gardens from this time are noteworthy for incorporating elaborate arrangements of rocks—many using colorful stones such as blue *aoishi*, brought from the island of Shikoku—and the introduction of exotic plants such as sago palms imported from the south.

Edo period (1600–1868)

Japan's sociopolitical climate was stabilized by a strong central government in Edo (now Tokyo) during this time. The long period of stability allowed for the mature development of many aspects of garden culture. Tea gardens developed into the form we see today. Extensive stroll gardens (*kaiyushiki-teien*) were built on the estates of the daimyo, and urban merchants began to build small courtyard gardens (*tsuboniwa*) in their townhouses.

Meiji period (1868–1912)

This period witnessed the opening of Japan's borders and the introduction of Western technology and culture as the emperor was restored and the feudal system abolished. The private stroll gardens of the daimyo were either destroyed or turned into public parks, such as Kenrokuen in Kanazawa, Korakuen in Okayama, and Rikugien in Tokyo.

Gardens to See in Japan

Brian Funk

For a true appreciation of the Japanese garden tradition, you must visit Japan. Some exemplary gardens are well-known tourist destinations; others are somewhat off the beaten path. The greatest array of historical gardens, as well as temples, castles, and other important cultural sites, can be found in or near the city of Kyoto, the former imperial capital, but many nice examples can also be found in Tokyo. Here are my favorite gardens to visit in Japan.

Katsura Imperial Villa, Nishikyoku

Often described as the quintessential example of Japanese taste, this grand 17th-century cultural treasure is just west of Kyoto. Modeled on the villa and gardens of the 11th-century classic *Tale of Genji*, it is a large stroll garden that includes several structures considered to be the greatest achievements of Japanese architecture. Tours are conducted only by permission from the Imperial Household Agency.

Murinan, Kyoto

This small villa and modest stroll garden is situated in the eastern hills of Kyoto and was created at the end of the 19th century by a former prime minister with famed garden designer Ogawa Jihei. Most public gardens in Kyoto are temple or imperial gardens, so this combination of house and garden is unusual. It features a small waterfall and a wide, shallow stream winding through an open lawn, with the borrowed scenery of the hills as a backdrop.

Tofukuji, Kyoto

An ancient Zen Buddhist temple located in southeastern Kyoto, Tofukuji includes modern gardens designed by Mirei Shigemori in the late 1930s. Their hybrid style combines Japanese tradition with Western influences. The checkerboard-patterned moss garden is perhaps most well known, though I think the *karesansui* next to the abbot's quarters (left) is even more impressive.

Adachi Museum of Art, Yasugi

Opened on the western coast of Japan in 1970, this complex of museum halls displays modern Japanese art and adjacent gardens. These include a massive karesansui, which can be viewed from the museum but not entered. Set against the surrounding mountains, it features vast gravel areas and hundreds of meticulously pruned trees and shrubs. Perhaps the only criticism that could be made is that the garden is too perfect.

Nijo Castle, Kyoto

This UNESCO World Heritage Site is a former shogun residence and imperial palace that includes boldly designed gardens within its 17th-century fortifications. The Ninomaru Palace garden was the tour de force of Kobori Enshu, a garden and tea master of that time. It consists of a pond with three islands and many upright stones set along the shoreline. Some say it's excessive, but I completely disagree.

Kenrokuen, Kanazawa

Kenrokuen, in western Japan, was originally developed in the Edo period by the Maeda clan, the local feudal lords, and was once part of the nearby Kanazawa Castle. Now a stroll garden, it has a large pond with a fountain and many twisting waterways. Its unique two-legged stone lantern is said to resemble a Japanese harp and has become a symbol for the garden itself.

Tokyo Gardens

Tokyo also has some very nice gardens. Several are large and parklike, including Koishikawa Korakuen, Kyu Shiba, Shinjuku Gyoen, and the fantastic Rikugien (right). For a more intimate experience, travel to the quaint Shibamata neighborhood to visit the beautiful modern courtyard garden and teahouse at Yamamototei. It offers a rare opportunity to see such a garden from within a house.

Japanese Gardens in the United States

Jeanne Rostaing

On the following pages you will find profiles of eight distinctive public Japanese gardens on U.S. soil. They are geographically diverse—representing both the east and west coasts and the middle of the country as well. Each has been adapted to its particular climate, and many have growing conditions quite different from those in Japan. Their stories also span a century of garden history in this country, starting with Brooklyn Botanic Garden's Japanese Hill-and-Pond Garden, which opened to the public in 1915.

Visiting an American Japanese garden is of course much different from visiting a garden in Japan, but the popularity of these places shows what a powerful attraction the Japanese gardening tradition holds for a Western audience. Brooklyn's garden and other older gardens opened to widespread admiration early in the 20th century, when Japanese culture was at the height of fashion. Over the years, the popularity of this garden style has waxed and waned, and many struggled before and during World War II. Later efforts to heal postwar relations between the United States and Japan helped to revive interest, paving the way for the restoration of older gardens and the creation of new ones.

Today there are hundreds of Japanese gardens in the United States, and Americans are as enamored of them as ever. Perhaps it is because they offer exquisite beauty in all seasons. Or maybe it's because they offer something simple and natural at a time when many of us feel bombarded by the choices of our technology-driven world. In a Japanese garden, we can take in the riches of the natural world sparingly, one gorgeous vista at a time. Here it is possible to calm the mind.

As you read about the eight gardens presented in this book, you will no doubt form your own opinion about why they draw us in. Maybe you will be intrigued enough to visit one or more of them. You may even come to understand why these places, traditionally hailed as educational examples of Japanese culture, seem to have become something more, something that offers us comfort and the opportunity for spiritual renewal.

The gate to the tea garden within the Portland Japanese Garden, one of the best-regarded Japanese-style gardens in the United States.

Urban Refuge

Pass through the tall wooden gates into the viewing pavilion of Brooklyn Botanic Garden's Japanese Hill-and-Pond Garden, and all at once you have left the hubbub of city life behind. Inside you'll find a sense of peace and serenity even when the garden is filled with visitors. Opened in 1915, this is one of the oldest extant Japanese-inspired gardens in the United States and the first to be built in a public botanic garden. More than a century later, it remains a testament to Americans' enduring appreciation of Japanese gardens.

Brooklyn's Japanese garden is a stroll garden into which elements of other traditional styles have been incorporated. It was designed to be both viewed from a distance and explored on foot. Upon entering the pavilion from the formal entrance, you first experience the garden as a vista, composed as a painter would compose a painting. To the left is a dramatic vermilion-colored wooden torii, a traditional gate signifying that a Shinto shrine lies beyond. It emerges from the pond against a background of gently rounded hills and a wooded path. To the right, an arched bridge leads to a small grassy island, where a Japanese black pine has been pruned to look windblown and contorted with age.

This idealized landscape was created in the Japanese tradition of *shizen*—the art of making a garden look as though it has grown that way on its own. Other vistas are gradually revealed as you walk along the garden's winding paths, including a five-tiered waterfall that you hear before you see as you round a bend. Farther on, a small rustic Shinto shrine sits on a steep hill.

Japanese style was very much in vogue when the garden's creator, Takeo Shiota, came to the United States from Japan in 1907. Japanese gardens had been exhibited in several recent world's fairs to popular acclaim, and they were being installed in

Japanese Hill-and-Pond Garden
bbg.org

LOCATION Brooklyn, New York   SIZE 3.5 acres

DESIGNER Takeo Shiota   OPENED 1915

STYLE modified stroll

NOTABLE FEATURES Shinto torii and shrine, wooden bridges, waterfall, waiting bench, teahouse-style viewing pavilion, 17th-century stone lantern

CULTURAL EVENTS Sakura Matsuri, *hanami*

museums and chic hotels as well as on the private estates of wealthy Americans. Shiota—who had resisted traditional apprenticeship and acquired his design sense by trekking alone on foot to study the Japanese landscape—had designed several residential gardens in the New York area by the time he was hired by Brooklyn Botanic Garden to design a garden for its developing site, in 1914.

Philanthropist Alfred T. White donated the relatively modest sum of $13,000 for the project, and Shiota set to work with a crew of laborers and horse-powered equipment. At the center of the garden was a 1½-acre pond, a remnant of the brief period when the site had been a park. Its winding, asymmetrical shape ensured that it could never be viewed in its entirety, so that the viewer must walk to see it from different perspectives.

Water flows into the pond on its western shore via Shiota's statuesque waterfall. Instead of the traditional rounded stones usually used in Japanese water features, it is composed of shelves of jagged Manhattan schist. The result was said by some to resemble an Italian grotto, and it is possible that the Italian workers assisting Shiota influenced its design, which also includes echo chambers to amplify the sound of falling water.

Shiota contoured the land around the pond into a series of steep hills and planted Japanese maples and flowering cherries along the shore, adding pines and other conifers around the pond. Japanese plants were rare in the United States at that time, so

This covered waiting bench is modeled after those on which guests would sit before being summoned for a traditional tea ceremony.

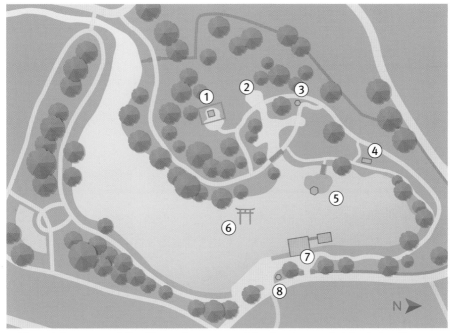

1 shinto shrine, 2 waterfall, 3 Kasuga lantern, 4 waiting bench, 5 turtle island, 6 torii,
7 viewing pavilion/main entrance, 8 Komatsu lantern

Shiota used a mix of Asian and native species in his design. When it opened in 1915, Shiota's finished garden was well received and enjoyed great popularity until just before World War II. In 1938 its shrine was burned down, and the garden was closed for a time due to public antipathy to Japan.

After the war, Japanese-American gardener Frank Okamura was hired to care for the garden. During his long tenure, he restored the garden, including the shrine, and helped develop BBG's world-renowned bonsai collection. In 1999, a $3 million restoration championed by BBG president Judith Zuk helped return the garden to Shiota's original vision. An enormous buildup of silt was removed from the pond, and the shoreline was renovated to prevent erosion. Taking over just as the infrastructure work was being completed, curator Brian Funk was able to select new plants for the garden, with an eye toward creating more authentic Japanese plantings over time.

Even as the plantings evolve, they reflect the Japanese goal of four-season interest, achieved through color and structure. The delicate Japanese maples are beautiful year-round, especially when their foliage turns brilliant shades of red and gold in the fall. Curator Funk, who studied gardening techniques in Japan, says that fully half of his work in the garden is pruning. Azaleas and other evergreen shrubs are shaped into gentle domes to provide important structure year-round. Since the trees and shrubs have been carefully pruned, they hold snow, expanding the garden's seasonal appeal.

The pavilion is modeled after a traditional teahouse, but it functions as a viewing platform from which visitors can admire the landscape.

Every spring, all of New York City eagerly awaits Brooklyn Botanic Garden's first cherry blossoms—usually those of *Prunus* 'Fudan-zakura' and *P. subhirtella* 'Pendula' on the shore of the pond. To celebrate *hanami*, the tradition of viewing cherry blossoms, visitors flock to the Garden over the next month as the rest of its famous collection of ornamental cherries blooms in the Japanese Hill-and-Pond Garden and the adjacent Cherry Esplanade and Cherry Walk. Each tree may be in bloom for only a week, but the sequence occurs over five weeks, and many people return frequently to catch the whole show.

The season culminates with Sakura Matsuri, a two-day festival to celebrate traditional and contemporary Japanese culture that attracts upwards of 70,000 people. This beloved rite of spring is a fitting way to introduce Shiota's garden to visitors and entice them to return over and over to delight in nature in the heart of the city.

Clockwise from top left: This 17th-century lantern was a gift from Tokyo. Great blue herons are frequent visitors. Turtles and koi inhabit the pond. A snow-viewing lantern, or *yukimigata-doro*, allows snow to collect on top. The mix of deciduous and evergreen plants creates gorgeous fall scenes. One of the garden's famed cherry cultivars (*Prunus subhirtella* 'Pendula') blooms along the pond's shore.

A Gilded Age Garden Endures

As you explore this extravagant 12-acre garden, you'll see iconic representations of the way Japanese garden design has been interpreted in the United States. Along with an original stroll garden, complete with moon bridge, koi ponds, stone lanterns, and wisteria arbor, there is a newer tea garden with an authentic teahouse, as well as a dramatic dry rock garden that leads to a bonsai display. Now a popular public attraction, the Huntington's Japanese Garden is also one of the few remaining examples of the many Japanese gardens that were designed for private estates at the turn of the 20th century, the heyday of America's fascination with all things Japanese.

This garden is part of the Huntington Library, Art Collections, and Botanical Gardens, created from the California estate of Henry E. Huntington, the Gilded Age railroad and real estate tycoon. Like many of his contemporaries, Huntington was enthralled with the idea of assembling collections of exotic plants and objets d'art, and those of Japan, in particular, were at the height of highbrow fashion.

Huntington's acquisition of a Japanese garden was jump-started by the failure of a commercial tea garden in nearby Pasadena. In 1903, businessman George T. Marsh built an attraction there similar to the tea garden he'd built in San Francisco for the 1894 World's Fair. Marsh's popular San Francisco garden still exists today, but his Pasadena project was a flop. In 1911, he was only too happy to sell to Huntington its complete collection of plants and artifacts, including a five-room Japanese house.

The contents of Marsh's garden were reassembled on a nine-acre site along a canyon at Huntington's San Marino ranch. His young, plant-loving foreman, William Hertrich, and a crew of 70 men prepared the area. They drained an old reservoir, graded the land, built concrete ponds and a waterfall, and hauled boulders from the nearby San Gabriel Mountains. With Huntington anxious to have

Japanese Garden at the Huntington
huntington.org

LOCATION **San Marino, California**   SIZE **12 acres**

DESIGNER **William Hertrich**   OPENED TO THE PUBLIC **1928**

STYLES **stroll, dry, tea**

NOTABLE FEATURES **moon bridge, 1911 Japanese house, teahouse, bamboo forest, bonsai court, viewing stones, dry rock garden**

CULTURAL EVENTS **tea ceremony demonstrations, plant sales, free lectures**

the garden finished for the arrival of Arabella, his new wife, Hertrich was obliged to work quickly.

In the spring of 1912, the house was reassembled and installed on site by master carpenter Toichiro Kawai, who had been a shipbuilder in Japan. Kawai also created a traditional bell tower, three wooden gates, and that familiar architectural element in American Japanese gardens, a moon bridge. Its high, rounded, arched shape forms a complete circle, reminiscent of the full moon, when viewed with its reflection in the water.

To build the bridge, Kawai used an extremely rare and ancient Chinese technique in which short pieces of straight wood are "woven" together to form a graceful curve. Originally, the bridge and other wooden structures built by Kawai were painted a bright vermilion. However, during a restoration in 1992, the paint was removed from the bridge, and today it has a natural wood finish thought to be more in keeping with the notion in Japanese design that materials, such as rocks, wood, and bamboo, should retain their natural appearance.

The trees purchased from Marsh included Japanese maples as well as conifers such as pine and cypress and fruit trees including plum, peach, and cherry. Hertrich had them boxed up and brought to San Marino by wagon. Azaleas, chrysanthemums, peonies, camellias, wisteria, and iris also came from the Marsh garden. Many of these plants have survived and still grace the Huntington today.

Henry Huntington's granddaughter Harriet and her tutor sit on the moon bridge circa 1918, when the garden was still part of the family's private estate.

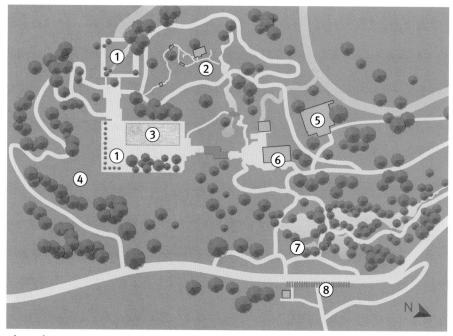

1 bonsai courts, 2 tea garden and teahouse, 3 dry garden, 4 bamboo forest, 5 ikebana house, 6 Japanese house, 7 moon bridge, 8 wisteria arbor

It wasn't until 1928, a year after Huntington's death, that the estate was opened to the public. Among the first public gardens in the Los Angeles area, it was immediately popular. But as the Great Depression took hold in the 1930s, funds for maintenance became scarce, and things quickly took a downward turn.

By the time World War II began, the Japanese Garden was already in poor condition. After the bombing of Pearl Harbor in 1941, the name of the garden was changed to the "Oriental Garden," but anti-Japanese sentiments led to further neglect and closure of some parts of the garden. By the late 1950s it was all but abandoned. Its buildings, including the Japanese house, in dramatic disrepair, were closed and facing possible demolition.

Help arrived in 1957 in the form of a group of local preservationists, the San Marino League. The league approached the Huntington with a plan to help restore the Japanese house, and within a year the volunteers had repaired and cleaned the interior and reopened the house. The building became a place where classes in Japanese flower arranging and tea ceremonies were held. The partnership between the Huntington and the San Marino League continued and led to further restoration and development.

Today, Henry Huntington's original stroll-style garden has been restored to its former glory. As in Huntington's day, you enter by walking through a wooden gate guarded by two stone lions. As you pass the vintage bell tower and the wisteria arbor, you get a sense of the founder's original vision, described as "Japanese-

American in an eclectic come-together" by Jim Folsom, the Telleen/Jorgensen Director of the Botanical Gardens at the Huntington. All of its elements—the moon bridge and koi ponds, banks of azaleas, twisty, cloud-pruned trees, stone pagoda lantern, and Japanese house—form a stylized antique Japanese village, the sort of scene you might see in a snow globe.

But if you continue on across a wooden zigzag bridge over a newly constructed waterfall, you will come upon more recent garden additions that have a distinctively different aesthetic. First there is the dramatic Zen Court. Built in 1968 by staff craftsmen, it contains a *karesansui*, a dry rock garden, and an adjoining series of outdoor rooms that display bonsai and a collection of viewing stones. These features exemplify an overall trend toward smaller and simpler gardens, with rocks and gravel representing the elements of a garden landscape.

Past the Zen Court is a rustic path up to *Seifu-an*, or the Arbor of Pure Breeze, a ceremonial teahouse sitting high upon a knoll. It was built in Kyoto and installed here in 2011. From inside, there are views of the new three-quarter-acre tea garden, with its stone lantern and Japanese maples, camellias, azaleas, and junipers set against a background of Himalayan cedars. Outside sits a waiting bench and gate that were created in Japan. The teahouse is often the setting for demonstrations of the traditional tea ceremony, part of the Huntington's continuing mission to promote Japanese culture.

A view of the original stroll garden includes the 1911 house and many elements of a typical early-20th-century American Japanese garden, like the moon bridge and pagoda lantern.

The Zen Court was created in 1968 and features viewing stones and greenery. In it, the garden's bonsai collection is displayed in a rotation to highlight seasonal interest.

Both the Zen Court and the teahouse reflect a shift in approach at the Huntington. Rather than reflect American interpretations of Japanese style, they were executed with a meticulous respect for ancient Japanese traditions and cultural accuracy. Together, the three different gardens within the garden offer a history of how America's relationship with the Japanese aesthetic has evolved. The stroll garden represents a quaint, early-20th-century idea of Japan, made by people who admired the country but didn't really understand its sensibilities. The decision to preserve it this way is deliberate, a way of educating visitors about how far our knowledge and appreciation of Japanese culture has come.

If Henry Huntington were to see his garden today he would no doubt be pleased. The artificial concrete boulders around his koi ponds have been carefully restored, and the purple wisteria is still blooming in front of the Japanese house, but the institution is evolving and thriving, and half a million people a year now come to admire what he started more than a century ago.

An Unlikely Garden Blooms in Maine

Its history reads like a rather outlandish but fascinating novel. The hero, a country innkeeper, owns some vacant swampland on an island in Maine. Nearby, a famous doyenne of garden design declares she will pull to pieces her own beloved garden. Suddenly, exotic azaleas and other rare specimens are in jeopardy. In the nick of time, the innkeeper steps in, and with the help of a friendly millionaire, creates a home for them. Interestingly, this home is a Japanese garden. But the innkeeper is not Japanese, and they are not Japanese plants. He has never been to Japan or, for that matter, had any formal training at all as a garden designer.

Thus the magical and unique Asticou Azalea Garden was born. Today a well-loved public strolling garden with many Japanese touches—a rustic stone lantern, an austere sand garden—it is primarily a flower garden, something most Japanese gardens are not. The azaleas here are not sheared into compact mounds. They are allowed to grow with wild abandon, delighting the many visitors who make a point of coming in late spring to see the masses of flowers.

The garden's creator, Charles K. Savage, descended from an old seafaring clan that had settled on the Maine coast in the late 1700s. The family owned the venerable Asticou Inn, a grand hotel on Mount Desert Island near Acadia National Park. After his father's death in 1922, Charles, 19 years old and the eldest son, was called home from college to take over the family business, which he then ran for virtually the rest of his life. Savage had an interest in garden design and loved Asian art. He had never been to Asia but was an enthusiastic armchair traveler and scholar and had read widely on Japan.

On the same island lived famed garden designer Beatrix Farrand, whose family summer home, Reef Point, overlooked Frenchman Bay. Farrand's high-profile career

Asticou Azalea Garden
gardenpreserve.org

LOCATION Northeast Harbor, Maine   SIZE 5 acres

DESIGNER Charles K. Savage   OPENED 1956

STYLES stroll, dry

NOTABLE FEATURES plant collection of renowned landscape designer Beatrix Farrand, pond, sand garden

had led her to design such enduring projects as the East Garden at the White House and the rose garden at Dumbarton Oaks in Washington, DC For her six-acre Reef Point property, she had created magnificent gardens filled with thousands of plants collected from all over the world. Her hope was to turn the site and her 2,700-volume horticulture library into an education center for nascent landscape architects. However, in 1955, when she was 73 and had failed to find financing for the center, Farrand made the radical decision to tear down her house, dismantle the gardens, and put the property up for sale.

Savage moved quickly to buy the plants, including rare azaleas and rhododendrons, a Sargent weeping hemlock tree, crabapple trees, and a unique Japanese cherry hybrid. But he lacked the funds for relocating them to his property. Fortunately, he counted among his friends the businessman and philanthropist John D. Rockefeller Jr., who was captivated by the project and contributed the needed money.

Once the plant collection had been secured, Savage set about creating a Japanese garden to showcase it. The site he selected was a swampy parcel crowded with weedy alders just west of the Asticou Inn. It also held a pond kept as a firefighting reservoir and used as an ice skating rink in winter.

Savage then devoted himself to creating the garden, and the project was complete in just a year's time. He hired local workers to articulate the edges of the pond, clear the alders, and fill in marshy land with topsoil. Gnarled native pitch pines,

Rather than being sheared into sculptural shapes, the azaleas at Asticou are allowed to grow naturally. In the late spring, a profusion of different cultivars are in bloom.

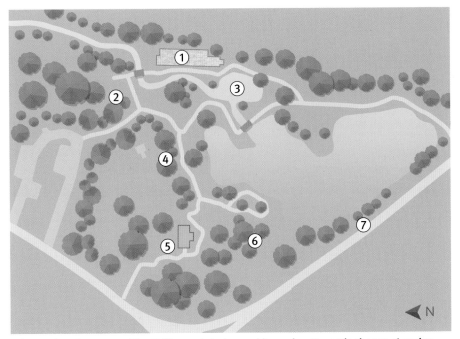

1 dry garden, 2 moss corridor, 3 lily pond, 4 streamside garden, 5 meetinghouse, 6 azalea mountainscape, 7 mugo pines

sometimes called natural bonsai, were brought in as well as chunks of local granite. Savage combed the beaches for the perfect accent stones and studied the carefully documented bloom times of the Farrand azaleas in order to place them to the greatest effect. He even searched the ruins of old estates for perfect design elements, such as a stone wall that was salvaged for the site.

A flat area inspired Savage to create a rock garden like one he had seen at the Museum of Fine Arts in Boston. He used large granite chunks to represent islands and raked quartz sand to represent the sea, a departure from the gravel usually used in *karesansui*. He even custom designed a wooden rake to maintain it. This dry garden remains the most distinct feature at Asticou and is carefully cleaned and raked weekly.

Now more than 50 years old, Asticou still retains its original stroll garden layout. After passing through the entrance gate, visitors follow a shady path through a traditional moss garden, where cushions of velvety green moss are interspersed with ferns in a lush woodland that flourishes in this humid seaside location.

The meandering paths take you around the lily pond, past a point jutting out into the pond and across the south bridge to the streamside garden. Over the years, more Japanese elements have been added to the garden, including five antique stone lanterns and a row of mugo pines that were planted along the roadside to add privacy to the garden and enhance the borrowed scenery.

Climate change has also altered the garden. In the long, harsh Maine winters of the past, the garden would remain dormant until late May and then suddenly burst

The dry garden features boulders of local granite and raked quartz sand, an unusual departure from the gravel typically used in Japanese *karesansui*.

into flower at the first sign of spring. Now the change is more gradual. When the blooms come, there are, as always, banks of pink flowers from crabapples and Farrand's pinkshell azaleas, natives of coastal North Carolina that thrive along the Maine coast. However, these blossoms are now accompanied by several yellow-flowered *Rhododendron* cultivars. Formerly unable to withstand Maine's brutal Zone 5 winters, they have been added to the garden now that Asticou's climate has warmed to USDA Zone 6.

The garden is also expanding. In 2005, an adjoining property was purchased along the western border, and an existing building was transformed into a meeting house with public restrooms. The three-acre expansion is being carefully merged with the original garden, and so subtle are the new plantings that it's hard to tell where the original garden stops and the new one starts. Pitch pines and granite rocks have been obtained from the same sources that Savage used back in the 1950s. No doubt he would be gratified to know that although Asticou, as well as our planet, is changing, the choices he made so long ago are still being honored and his beautiful garden continues to delight its many visitors.

Asticou's renowned azalea collection includes specimens originally obtained from Beatrix Farrand's estate as well as newer cultivars. Clockwise from top left: yellow hybrid azalea (*Rhododendron* 'Hong Kong'), Japanese azalea (*R. japonicum*), plumleaf azalea (*R. prunifolium*), Ghent hybrid azalea (*R. × gandavense*).

Important Elements in Japanese-Inspired Gardens

Sarah Schmidt

In Japan, gardens are considered to be distilled versions of the natural world, so plants and other elements play different roles from those Westerners expect in a garden. Understanding the traditional ways in which these elements have been used will deepen your appreciation of the gardens in which they are found.

Rocks

Rocks are sometimes said to be the "bones of the earth" and provide structure in a garden. Arrangements of large boulders may be used to represent particular landscape features like mountains or islands, or they may be used as sculptural elements based on their shape, texture, and color. Setting stones is considered an important art in Japanese gardening, and the way they are placed establishes balance and a sense of harmony.

Water

Water represents renewal and is often included in ways that mimic natural water features. For instance, large stroll gardens usually include a pond or stream. Many gardens also feature waterfalls that create pleasing natural sounds to help insulate the setting from a noisy environment. In dry gardens, water is represented by gravel raked to evoke waves.

Evergreens

In Japanese gardens, plants are valued for their year-round beauty, and there's much less focus on spring and summer flowers than in typical Western gardens. Pines and other evergreens represent permanence and consistency in nature and are usually featured heavily. They are frequently pruned to appear weathered, since age and perseverance are valued in Japanese culture. Japanese gardens also tend to contain a simple palette with fewer types of plants than Western gardens.

Flowers and Foliage

Many plants are chosen for the way they showcase the beauty of the changing seasons. Flowering plants are included for their ephemeral beauty and seasonal significance. Rather than beds of annuals, though, Japanese gardens usually include flowering trees and shrubs like cherries, plums, azaleas, and camellias, which display flowers and sometimes fruit. These are often selected with an eye toward creating an ongoing display, so a variety of cultivars with different bloom times may be included. Likewise, plants with dramatic fall foliage, like Japanese maples, are also featured.

Architecture

In Japan, gardens are considered an extension of the home or another structure and are valued for the way they bring nature into everyday life. Indoor and outdoor spaces are closely integrated, and enclosed landscapes are often created just beyond a sliding door or large window. Buildings frequently include internal courtyard gardens that are viewed from inside but not entered. In North America, many display gardens include structures like homes or teahouses to showcase a particular architecture and garden style together.

Ornaments

Most garden objects have traditionally served practical purposes in Japan—lanterns were originally included to provide light; water basins were included as a place to wash in preparation for a tea ceremony. In North America, ornaments like these are often included to suggest a particular traditional style of garden. However, some of the most authentic Japanese-style gardens here have few or no ornaments at all.

Bridges, Gates, and Paths

Likewise, bridges, gates, and paths are often included in American Japanese gardens to showcase a particular style, but most of these styles originated in Japan to serve a certain purpose. Zigzag bridges, for example, were once simple plank arrangements formed as a practical way to cross a stream, and the gates in a tea garden were designed to help the visitor feel that the outside world has been left behind.

Beautiful Friendship

To wander the lush, winding paths of the Portland Japanese Garden is to get an education in the beauty of Japanese garden styles over the ages. This "sampler" garden includes five styles from different periods in Japan's thousand-year history of formal garden design. It's also a lovely representation of a more modern tradition: It was created in the 1960s as part of a historic 20th-century effort to promote international harmony and cooperation.

Once you've ascended the steep hill to the garden's entry gate, you enter a world far removed from the city of Portland, a separation that illustrates a key tenet of Japanese design—breaking the connection with the outside world. The garden inside includes many classical motifs. Some of the most dramatic views are borrowed; stones are carefully placed as symbols; and seemingly aimless paths are anything but.

Just inside the entry gate is a stone water basin, a traditional symbol of cleansing. Ahead, leading the way into the first of the five smaller gardens, is a wisteria arbor framing an imposing, century-old stone pagoda lantern. The 18-foot-tall lantern was a gift in 1963 from the mayor of Sapporo, Portland's sister city in Japan since 1958.

In the aftermath of World War II, the U.S. government actively promoted the rebuilding of cultural ties with Japan and promoted a sister-city initiative through which Portland and Sapporo were brought together. A surge of interest in Japanese culture followed and inspired Portland city leaders to establish a Japanese garden. Soon after, the newly established Japanese Garden Society of Oregon selected a site 500 feet above sea level in the West Hills, overlooking the city and in sight of Mount Hood, sometimes called the Mount Fuji of North America. The group hired internationally known Japanese landscape designer Takuma Tono, a professor at the Tokyo Agricultural University who had studied at Cornell University. Tono, who came to the

Portland Japanese Garden
japanesegarden.com

LOCATION Portland, Oregon   SIZE 5.5 acres

DESIGNER Takuma Tono   OPENED 1967

STYLES stroll, tea, flat, dry, contemporary

NOTABLE FEATURES pagoda lantern, traditional teahouse, moon bridge

CULTURAL EVENTS art exhibitions, lectures on techniques such as bamboo fence building and pine pruning, ikebana displays

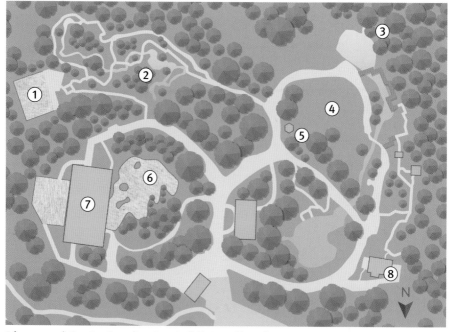

1 *karesansui*, 2 natural garden, 3 waterfall, 4 stroll garden, 5 stone pagoda lantern, 6 flat garden, 7 pavilion, 8 teahouse and tea garden

U.S. in 1963 for the initial phases of construction, was given a crew of city workers and 5½ acres of land that had once been the site of the Washington Park Zoo.

The garden opened officially in the summer of 1967, and in its long history has grown from a summer attraction with fewer than 30,000 annual visitors to a year-round institution that welcomes approximately 300,000 people a year. It has been widely praised for its authenticity, which may be attributed to the fact that the garden has always had supervisors from Japan who have adhered as closely as possible to Tono's vision.

Tono's plan in Portland included a quintet of distinct styles. He was, after all, a teacher of landscape architecture, so it makes sense that he wanted to provide Americans with as many examples as possible. He repurposed much of the existing zoo landscape to create water features and other garden elements.

Past the Sapporo lantern, you bear right along a tunnel of camellias leading to the moon bridge and Strolling Pond Garden. Here the paths alternately hide and reveal a series of vistas, including views of two large pools, the lower one the site of the old zoo's bear pit and the upper one the aviary. They are connected by a stream that flows over rocks trucked in from the Sandy River on the western slope of Mount Hood. A waterfall flows into the koi-filled lower pond from what was once the hibernation den for the zoo's bears. Irises bloom here in the spring, and Japanese holly and skimmia grow along the edges of the stream.

This stroll garden wraps around the Tea Garden, where an inner garden can be viewed from a traditional wooden teahouse when its shoji doors are slid open.

Called Kashintei ("Flower Heart Room"), the teahouse was a special project of Tono's. He persuaded garden officials to have it built in Japan, where an ancient tongue-in-groove wooden peg construction method was still in use. The house was then disassembled, shipped to Portland, and rebuilt by a Japanese carpenter over several weeks in 1968.

Above these two gardens lies the Natural Garden, an area originally designed by Tono as a moss garden and planted with native species from Mount Hood. Despite diligent care by the gardeners, it proved impossible to maintain, so in the 1970s, landscape designers Hachiro Sakakibara and Hoichi Kurisu (later the designer of the Anderson Japanese Gardens in Rockford, Illinois, and Roji-en in Delray Beach, Florida) transformed the garden by creating a large pond and planting azaleas, rhododendrons, pieris, and pines.

Among the five gardens, this one, with its looser style of pruning, waterfalls, and little bridges, is the most contemporary in appearance. However, it still makes ingenious use of the traditional hide-and-reveal concept. The twists and turns of the walkways and stairs bring new views every few steps. It is planted mainly with deciduous plants, such as Japanese maples and native vine maples, arranged to feature seasonal change. Over time, the trees have grown so tall that this spot is now cool and shady, allowing moss to flourish on its stones and pathways in much the way it was originally meant to.

The authentic wooden teahouse looks out onto a tea garden. The house was built in Japan using traditional tongue-in-groove carpentry and reassembled on-site.

Clockwise from top left: The Natural Garden was created in the 1970s and is an example of the more contemporary *zokinoniwa* garden style. The Flat Garden includes raked gravel and plants and is meant to be viewed rather than entered. The bridge in the stroll garden is surrounded by dramatic foliage in autumn. The dry garden exemplifies the Japanese principle of seeing the beauty of blank space.

The garden is located in the West Hills of Portland. It overlooks the city and offers magnificent views of Mount Hood, sometimes called the Mount Fuji of North America.

Adjacent to the Natural Garden and reached by a curving set of steps is the Sand and Stone Garden, a traditional *karesansui*, or dry garden, in which sand or gravel is carefully raked into patterns to stand in for water and stones replace the plants. Tono based the design of this garden on a 2,000-year-old Indian fable in which an incarnation of the Buddha sacrifices himself to save a starving tigress and her cubs, but the placement of the weathered stones on the white granite sand gives only the most subtle suggestion of the tale. It's a lovely example of the Japanese principle of seeing the beauty of blank space, or *ma*.

Portland's garden has been lauded as the most authentic Japanese garden outside of Japan, and there is no doubt that it continues to provide an impressive display of horticulture, meticulously maintained for optimum beauty in all seasons. But perhaps its most important achievement is in carrying out its designer's philosophy of a garden's true purpose. As Tono wrote, "A Japanese garden is not only a place for the cultivation of trees and flowering shrubs, but one that provides secluded leisure, rest, repose, meditation, and sentimental pleasure."

Labor of Love

One of the most highly regarded examples of contemporary Japanese garden design in this country, Anderson Japanese Gardens has evolved over 30 years from the residential garden of a Midwestern businessman to an expansive 14-acre public garden that draws thousands of visitors each week during its peak season.

In 1966, John Anderson was a young man recently out of college when he first traveled to Japan for the first time and fell in love with the country and its culture. "I visited the Temple of the Golden Pavilion in Kyoto, and the gardens there left an incredible impression on me," he says. A few years later, Anderson visited the Portland Japanese Garden and was inspired to create a garden of his own on the grounds of his Rockford, Illinois, home.

In 1978, he hired Hoichi Kurisu, who had just left his position as director at the Portland garden to start his own landscape design firm. It was the beginning of an enduring collaboration between the two. "The year we began work, I asked John how much time would be involved. He looked at me and shrugged his shoulders. Well, that was more than 30 years ago, and we are still at work," says Kurisu.

Since it was built on private property with only the wishes of its creators to drive the schedule, this garden has had the advantage of being developed over time. Anderson acquired more land by buying adjoining parcels as they became available. The garden has now reached 14 acres.

Initially Kurisu and Anderson began in a traditional mode by building a stroll garden around a natural spring-fed pond on the north side of the site. This portion of the garden includes American interpretations of such classical elements as a zigzag bridge surrounded by irises, a stream with a waterfall, a viewing pavilion, a moon bridge, and a crane island.

Anderson Japanese Gardens
andersongardens.org
LOCATION Rockford, Illinois
SIZE 14 acres
DESIGNER Hoichi Kurisu
ESTABLISHED 1978
STYLES stroll, dry, tea, contemporary
NOTABLE FEATURES guesthouse, teahouse, 60-foot waterfall, event pavilion
CULTURAL EVENTS summer festival, Tuesday garden evenings, tea ceremonies

The second phase was executed in a more relaxed, natural style, centered on a traditional Japanese guesthouse built in 1985 by Masahiro Hamada, a master of the *sukiya* architectural style. The elegant two-story house is reached from the pond garden via a number of paths winding through a woodland. Its full-length windows look onto a flat gravel garden, exemplifying a key goal of Japanese residential garden design—to seamlessly bring the landscape into the home.

In 1988, Anderson and Kurisu undertook their most spectacular engineering feat: the creation of a 60-foot waterfall and stone wall. It was constructed from 750 tons of rock, including a single boulder that weighed 21 tons. "Hoichi and I would go boulder hunting in southeastern Wisconsin in search of just the right rock for the right place. We would go to quarries and to farm fields, knocking on the farmers' doors to ask for permission for unwanted boulders," Anderson says.

Current curator Tim Gruner arrived at Anderson in 1989 and was part of the crew that built the 40-foot lower falls. Kurisu came to the site for three two-week stretches to personally direct the work, which was extremely complicated and involved careful rigging to safely arrange the heavy stones. Gruner says he was amazed by Kurisu's sense of three-dimensional space. Instead of working from a detailed plan, Kurisu was able to make placement decisions as the work progressed, telling Gruner that "one boulder informs the next."

The small teahouse is tucked beneath a canopy of deciduous trees, along a stream. This rustic retreat was created in a naturalistic style during a later phase of the garden's design.

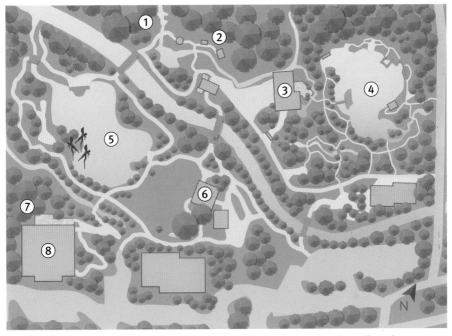

1 waterfall, 2 tea garden and teahouse, 3 guesthouse and dry garden, 4 stroll garden, 5 Garden of Reflection, 6 event pavilion, 7 *karesansui*, 8 visitor center

Also built during this phase was a teahouse with a waiting bench. The two features are a study in contrasts. The waterfall is dramatic, clamorous, and stimulating while the little teahouse, with oak trees arching over it and a man-made stream trickling by, is a quiet haven of repose.

In 1998, Anderson and his wife decided to open the garden to the public and donated it to the not-for-profit Rockford Rotary Charitable Association. That year also saw the addition of a four-acre site that features a visitor center as well as a *karesansui*, or dry garden, and the contemporary-style Garden of Reflection, which meets Americans with Disabilities Act standards. There is also a lawn and a 2,500-square-foot open-air pavilion that attracts hundreds of visitors each week for summertime music series, weddings, and other public and private events.

A garden as large as Anderson requires an enormous amount of care. Gruner estimates that half of his work is pruning. Many of the evergreens have been carefully shaped for 35 years, and the garden's Japanese maples as well as Amur maples, a hardy understory tree with beautiful form, also need regular tending. Formal pruning, in which trees are trimmed to look older and windswept, is used on the pines in some areas, but many trees are shaped in a looser, more natural style. That is especially true near the teahouse and guesthouse, which are meant to be rustic retreats.

Anderson and Kurisu are still actively involved with the garden and are looking forward to the continuing development of their creation. Both have been honored

Pruned evergreens are among the trees flanking the pond of the Garden of Reflection. The floating deck provides a peaceful spot to sit and relax.

for their work, each, notably, by the country of the other. In 1988, Kurisu received a National Landscape Award at the White House from First Lady Nancy Reagan. Anderson received a silver cup from the Japanese government as well as the Order of the Rising Sun in honor of his work promoting friendship and mutual understanding between the United States and Japan.

The future of Anderson Japanese Gardens will be determined by the continued teamwork of these two men and by their meticulous attention to detail. As Kurisu explains, "We continue to enjoy ourselves after all this time because we are not out to create something for our own glory or pride. We have created something purely from the heart, and we want to nurture it."

Clockwise from top left: The *sukiya*-style guesthouse has full-length windows that integrate the outdoor and indoor space. The zigzag bridge with irises is one of the classic elements in the original portion of the garden. A dry rock garden can be seen from the guesthouse. A cypress bridge spans the stream and leads from the waterfall to the Garden of Reflection.

A Midwestern Garden of Islands

Of all the Japanese gardens in the United States, the Elizabeth Hubert Malott Japanese Garden at the Chicago Botanic Garden most seems to resemble the coast of Japan. It consists of three islands, and virtually every view includes water. It is this garden's defining element.

In fact, nearly the entire Chicago Botanic Garden, which opened in 1972, was built on a series of islands in a lake. The 17-acre Japanese garden, also known as Sansho-En, or "Garden of Three Islands," was dedicated in 1982, and its designer, renowned landscape designer Koichi Kawana, used the island geography to great effect.

Sansho-En is entered via an arched wooden bridge. In a typical stroll garden, you walk around the edge of a pond or lake while your gaze is directed inward to scenes in and across the water. In Sansho-En, this tradition is turned on its head, and you travel around the perimeter of the islands looking outward onto the lake and other islands. Scenes are revealed, then hidden, and then perhaps revealed again from a different perspective farther along the winding paths.

The first island is Keiunto, "Island of the Auspicious Cloud." Here formally pruned pines and shaped evergreen shrubs line the path and shore. A modern granite zigzag bridge takes you over to the island of Seifuto, which has a less formal design. The plants here are not pruned as aggressively and appear more naturalistic. From here, you also have views of the third island, Horaijima, or "Island of Everlasting Happiness," which represents a paradise inaccessible to ordinary mortals. Visitors can only gaze at it across the water from afar.

Water as a design element, of course, does not have to be literally represented. Kawana created two dry gardens in Sansho-En. The one on Keiunto is near the *shoin* house, built in 1981 by Japanese craftsmen in the traditional style typical of retreats

Sansho-En: The Elizabeth Hubert Malott Japanese Garden
chicagobotanic.org

LOCATION Glencoe, Illinois

SIZE 17 acres

DESIGNER Koichi Kawana

OPENED 1982

STYLES stroll, dry

NOTABLE FEATURES *shoin* house, dry gardens, arbors, granite zigzag bridge, remote paradise island

CULTURAL EVENTS family days, children's festival, summer festival

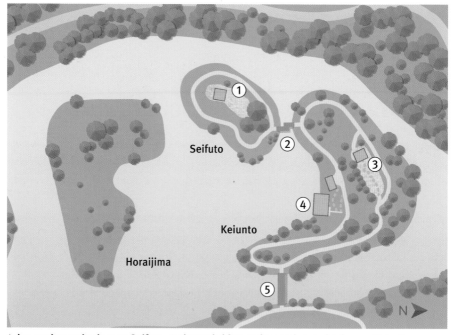

1 dry garden and arbor on Seifuto, 2 zigzag bridge, 3 dry garden and arbor on Keiunto, 4 *shoin* house, 5 arched bridge

used by daimyo (feudal lords). Though the main house is not accessible to the public, the walls are open and the guides lead people into the *engawa*, or waiting area, and explain the house's history, classic design, and traditional construction.

The second dry garden is on Seifuto and is situated by an arbor that was built in Japan, inspired by a Buddhist temple. It features an umbrella ceiling and a thatched, triangular roof. Kris Jarantoski, executive vice president and director of the botanic garden, says the arbor, with its views of the dry garden and the remote island of Hiraijima, is one of his favorite spots. He was there with Kawana the day that the designer named the island Seifuto. The weather was hot, and Kawana, accustomed to the milder climate of California, was grateful for the relief of a gentle wind. It was then that he declared the place Seifuto, "Island of Clear, Pure Breezes."

Kawana, who designed Japanese gardens across the country, including ones in St. Louis, Memphis, Los Angeles, and Denver, had a reputation for hands-on involvement. Although he provided drawings of his design for Sansho-En, Kawana also spent much time on-site, ensuring that the details of the garden were implemented according to his intentions. Jarantoski, who arrived at the botanic garden in 1977, remembers seeing him at the construction site, personally directing the placement of boulders.

Kawana believed that adhering to Japanese design principles and aesthetics was extremely important and even went so far as to source and place the ornaments in the garden. His approach to adornment was very conservative—he felt that objects should only be added if they served a purpose. A stone lantern, for instance, was only appropriate where light would be needed, perhaps beside a stairway.

Rather than use Japanese plants exclusively, Kawana chose a mix of Asian and native species based primarily on their ability to thrive in the Chicago area climate. For example, there are very few ornamental cherry trees at Sansho-En because they do not grow well in Chicago's harsh winters and heavy clay soil. There are, however, weeping willow trees flourishing near the water.

There are also Scots pines, some pruned formally, as well as azaleas, boxwood, and viburnum shrubs sheared into gentle mounds. Even after the garden was finished, Kawana continued to visit for years to advise on its development. Before he died, in 1990, Kawana taught Jarantoski to prune in the Japanese style, a skill he in turn has passed on to other horticulturists.

As in most public Japanese gardens, the maintenance at Sansho-En is intensive, constant, and therefore, expensive. In 2006, the garden was honored with an endowment for maintenance from the family of the late Elizabeth Hubert Malott, a Chicago woman who was a great fan of Sansho-En. In honor of that gift, the garden was rededicated in her name.

Kawana believed in placing ornaments where they would serve a logical purpose. This lantern sits beside an irregular path (left). Stepping stones lead through the raked gravel dry garden adjacent to the thatched-roof arbor (right).

Six Common Myths Debunked

Douglas Roth

The Japanese garden world is riddled with misinformation. Sadly, many inaccuracies are repeated so often that they become treated as facts. One researcher may hear a dubious story and mention it in his book about Japan. Then a second author repeats the same story and footnotes the first. Soon myth becomes fact. Or at least it does until we better educate ourselves.

Even the very term "Japanese garden" can be problematic. The tradition of creating gardens based on natural patterns and human sensory perception may have developed in Japan, but these concepts are not owned by any one country or culture. Architecture and interior spaces are also key components, so the word "garden" is not really comprehensive enough. I think the term "sukiya living environment" is more accurate, and I use the term "sukiya-style garden" to refer to the outdoor portion of that environment. (The word *sukiya* means teahouse style.) Other misunderstandings involve religion, symbolism, and China. Confusion also arises when Westerners confuse landscape gardening with bonsai. Learn to recognize some of these common myths.

Myth: Japanese gardens are religious places in which to meditate.
Japan is arguably the most secular nation on earth, and the sukiya-style garden has little or nothing to do with religion. It is true that both Shintoism and Buddhism place a lot of emphasis on nature, but neither religion has influenced Japan's garden tradition to the extent that many Americans believe.

You'll often see Japanese-style gardens and certain elements in them erroneously described as "inspired by Shintoism or Buddhism." The term "Zen garden" is also common and similarly misguided. (Please use the term "dry garden" instead.) In Japan, landscaping does exist at religious facilities, but it is just that: handsome landscaping. There is nothing inherently religious about it. The same style of gardens exist elsewhere in Japan, including at inns, restaurants, and private homes.

Myth: Each element in the garden has a symbolic meaning.
This is not true either. Most elements in a Japanese garden are meant to enhance the natural effect and help create a pleasant, comfortable mood. Odd stories about symbolism or superstition *detract* from that desired mood. There is certainly no need to make up (or repeat) unfounded stories about rocks, bridges, and so forth. And although intentional romantic fabrications are not unheard of, this practice does not reflect tradition.

Myth: Japan's garden traditions have their true origins in China.
The Japanese people deserve credit for their own cultural achievements. It's true that Chinese culture has had some influence on Japan, but that influence has been exaggerated—especially in regard to gardens. In fact, the sukiya tradition has nothing to do with China. It was developed in Japan—by Japanese craftsmen—largely during the Edo period, when outside influence on traditional arts was minimal.

Japanese gardens are not inherently religious. Statuary like this would be atypical in a public garden in Japan.

Myth: Japanese gardens don't have any turf or flowers.

In Japan, most of the very best sukiya-style gardens (for instance those at the Adachi Museum of Art and Katsura Imperial Villa) feature significant expanses of lawn. And while it is true that sukiya-style gardens don't have the large beds of flowering herbaceous plants that many Westerners are used to, they do feature flowering trees and shrubs that help ensure year-round color and four-season beauty.

Myth: Garden trees must be trained using ropes, braces, or wires.

It's true that trees and shrubs are pruned every year to keep them the right size and shape and sometimes to enhance the tree's character. But the shaping is done using hand pruning. Mechanical devices such as ropes, wires, and braces are generally not used. This myth probably came about as a result of Westerners conflating Japanese landscape gardening and bonsai, in which wires are used to shape trees.

Myth: Japanese gardens are miniaturized replicas of larger scenes.

The size of the trees and shrubs, as well as the size and layout of the entire garden, are all kept to a more *human scale*, so that we may experience the garden in a more intimate way. Garden elements are not shrunken down like the windmills in a miniature golf course but rather are maintained at a size that suits the human body and allows us to experience them with all five senses. Japanese pines, for instance, can reach 60 feet, but they are typically pruned to remain only about 12 feet tall so that we can better appreciate their unique details and overall form.

Tropical Twist

Nearly four decades after Takuma Tono created his sampler of five traditional Japanese gardens in Portland, Oregon, Hoichi Kurisu did him one better at the Morikami Museum in Delray Beach, Florida. Kurisu's creation, Roji-En: Garden of Drops of Dew, contains six gardens. Each is based on a style from Japan's long history and adapted for a tropical climate as well as to modern ideas about accessibility.

Unlike older Japanese gardens in the United States, Roji-En, which opened in 2001, was built to the specifications of the Americans with Disabilities Act (ADA). Thus this 16-acre garden is toured via a wide, flat path about a mile long. There is only one feature—a hillside meditation pavilion reached by steps—that is not completely accessible. Everywhere else, the gravel walkway accommodates visitors of all levels of mobility.

The gardens are entered through the newer of the two museum buildings on the grounds. The institution's mission is to educate Americans about Japanese culture, and this structure contains galleries, a theater, a research library, classrooms, a shop, and a café with waterside dining.

To explore Roji-en, the visitor crosses a traditional cypress bridge outside the museum and enters the *shinden* garden, the first of the six historic gardens. It's based on a style of palace garden of the Heian period (794–1185), the dawn of Japanese garden design and a time when Chinese influence was still very strong. Created for aristocrats, these gardens were meant to be viewed from boats, and Kurisu's version spans two islands created from a spit of land in the pond.

The shinden garden blends into the paradise garden, based on the earliest type of stroll garden, in which the visitor walks around a pond or lake on a path revealing changing vistas. Next are three examples of *karesansui* (dry rock garden) that illustrate

Roji-En: Garden of Drops of Dew
morikami.org

LOCATION Delray Beach, Florida   SIZE 16 acres

DESIGNER Hoichi Kurisu   OPENED 2001

STYLES *shinden*, early stroll, dry, modern

NOTABLE FEATURES lanterns, cypress bridge, bamboo grove, tropical and native plants

CULTURAL EVENTS New Year's celebration, spring Hatsume Fair, lantern festival

the style's evolution through several historical periods. The tour ends with the modern garden, a dramatic departure from the dry gardens. It is filled with plants adapted to a subtropical climate and inspired by the naturalistic style popular in early 20th-century Japan.

These six gardens are based on traditional designs but are not replicas. Rather, they are contemporary interpretations using plants suited to the local climate, says Heather Grzybek, who supervises the gardeners at Morikami. Most plants typical of Japanese gardens cannot tolerate Florida's summers, so Kurisu chose attractive plants that would thrive in hot, humid weather. For example, in the shinden garden, visitors will see gardenias, thunbergia vines, powderpuff trees, and other flowering species native to the tropics and subtropics.

Kurisu reworked the shoreline of the natural pond to create pleasing vistas and planted the area with native Florida slash pines, as well as juniper, tabebuia, and olive trees. Native Florida bald-cypress trees, which drop their leaves in December, provide some seasonal change.

There are other accommodations to the region too. No boulders are to be had in flat, sandy Florida, so tons of pale pink granite were brought in from Texas. Kurisu personally supervised the placement of each rock in the garden. Many have since shifted in the sandy soil over the years, some by as much as several feet. Occasional hurricanes require the staff to secure benches and other potential projectiles. An advantage of the

Wide, flat paths make the garden accessible to people of all abilities (left). Tropical plants like starburst (*Clerodendrum quadriloculare*) thrive here (right).

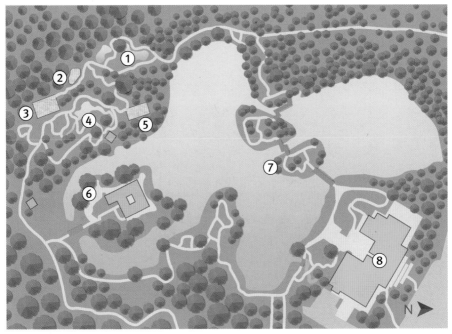

1 paradise garden, 2 early rock garden, 3 *karesansui*, 4 modern romantic garden, 5 flat garden, 6 bonsai walk, 7 *shinden* garden, 8 museum galleries and visitor center

Japanese style of pruning is that shrubs and trees sustain minimal damage from strong winds, which tend to blow through their manicured branches without resistance.

Wildlife is abundant at Morikami. Birds such as cormorant-like anhingas, great blue herons, and cattle egrets are spotted frequently, as are iguanas, bobcats, and turtles. Alligators often show up, too, but are not considered dangerous unless they are over six feet long, in which case the local parks department, which maintains the garden, can have them removed.

How south Florida should come to have a major Japanese garden in the first place is a curious story that began over a century ago. In 1903, a young Japanese man named Jo Sakai visited Florida and was inspired to start a utopian farming community to develop innovative growing techniques.

He named his project Yamato, an ancient name for Japan, and recruited other young, single Japanese men to live and work here. For a time they grew pineapples but were ultimately forced out of business by competition from Cuban growers. The young men drifted away and the colony disappeared, except for one person.

George Sukeji Morikami remained in Florida and ultimately made a fortune through farming, real estate, and a wholesale fruit and vegetable business. Near the end of World War II, he began buying land in the pinewoods near Delray Beach. As the years passed, Morikami, who had no family, tried to give his property to the local municipality, but land at the time was plentiful and cheap, and it wasn't until 1973 that Palm Beach County finally accepted the gift. Morikami lived to see the

The garden is the site of a number of cultural events, including a traditional Japanese lantern festival, in which the spirits of the departed are represented by paper lanterns.

beginning of construction on the 200-acre park and museum, which today preserve the history of Yamato and bear his name.

Construction of Roji-En began in 1993, only three years after the ADA was signed into law. Instead of finding the new regulations burdensome, Kurisu, who has long embraced the psychological and spiritual benefits of gardens, made accessibility an integral part of his design, a practical asset that only adds to its beauty.

The garden places a special focus on wellness and healing and hosts Stroll for Well-Being, a program of guided imagery walks for people living with post-traumatic stress disorder, grief, and depression. It's a fitting manifestation of Kurisu's belief that contact with the natural world is essential to mental, physical, and spiritual balance. At Morikami, the gates have been thrown open, generously offering the restorative power of nature to everyone.

Roji-En includes smaller gardens that each reference a different traditional style. Clockwise from top left: the early rock garden; the flat garden; the *shinden* garden; the paradise garden.

Natural Wonder

The four-acre Garden of the Pine Wind fits so neatly in its place that it seems to have always been there. But it is actually one of the newest Japanese gardens in the United States and a fine example of Japanese garden principals working in harmony with the local landscape. The creation of American garden designer David Slawson, it is located within Garvan Woodland Gardens, a large botanic garden built on restored land that was once clear-cut for timber.

The magic of Slawson's design is that it seems both extraordinary and completely natural. Visitors explore this stroll garden via a half-mile ADA-accessible path that gently winds down the steep hillside across two bridges, over a rushing man-made stream, past a dramatic 12-foot waterfall and smaller cascades that seem to be everywhere. Slawson has added some surprises along the way—secondary pathways lead to overlooks and water features not visible from the main path.

Slawson made use of the existing canopy of native black pine trees, now about 100 years old, and an understory of oak, hickory, and short-leaf pine. Flowering trees and shrubs like cherries, azaleas, native plums, and dogwoods, as well as tree peonies, put on a colorful show in the spring. In the summer, the garden appears in a more subdued palette of subtle greens.

Autumn visitors will see the brilliantly colored foliage of more than 60 varieties of maple. This is also when the fall-blooming azaleas put on their second act. These hybrid cultivars bloom twice each year, in the spring and then again in the fall, when their lavender, pink, and coral flowers mingle unexpectedly with the blazing fall woodland.

Despite its natural feel, the Garden of the Pine Wind is the result of years of hard work as well as some interesting turns of fate. The 200-acre site on Lake Hamilton where Garvan Woodland Gardens now sits had been stripped of timber in about

Garden of the Pine Wind
garvangardens.org

LOCATION Hot Springs, Arkansas   SIZE 4 acres

DESIGNER David Slawson   OPENED 2001

STYLE stroll

NOTABLE FEATURES stone moon bridge, wooden Sunrise Bridge, 12-foot waterfall, streams, smaller waterfalls

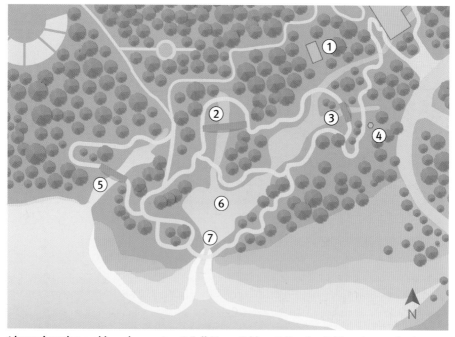

1 bonsai garden and learning center, 2 Full Moon Bridge, 3 Sunrise Bridge, 4 snow lantern, 5 Floating Cloud Bridge, 6 koi pond, 7 waterfall

1915 and then purchased in the 1920s by businessman Arthur Cook, who intended to log it again when the new trees matured. But in 1934, he was killed in an automobile accident, leaving his companies and properties to his wife and daughters. Though her mother and sister wanted nothing to do with them, 23-year-old Verna stepped up and steered the businesses safely through the Depression.

But Verna Cook wasn't just a businesswoman, she was also a nature lover. She became enamored with the parcel of land and decided that no more trees would be harvested. Over the years, she taught herself to be a gardener, diligently studying her huge collection of plant books. Soon she began adding ornamental plants to the property, at first with the idea of creating a grand private estate. Even after that plan was abandoned, she continued to develop the site. In the early 1980s, she visited San Francisco's Japanese Tea Garden in Golden Gate Park and was inspired to add a similar garden to her property.

Eventually Cook, now married and named Verna Cook Garvan, decided to share her land with the public. In 1985 she deeded the property to the University of Arkansas with the proviso that its landscape architecture program develop a botanic garden and operate it in perpetuity. Six years after her death in 1993, ground was broken. The first area to be developed was the Garden of the Pine Wind.

One of the most surprising features of this Japanese garden is the lack of traditional ornaments like lanterns and water basins. This was a deliberate choice by Slawson, based on his view that such objects don't have the same cultural context in the United States as they do in Asia. The only Japanese ornament he permitted in the garden was a stone snow lantern, donated by officials of Hot Springs' sister city of Hanamaki, Japan.

Because the design was based on the site's topography and doesn't have many overt Asian touches, it is an excellent example of the use of Japanese design principles adapted to, not imposed on, a garden site. There are other ways that this is a very local garden. The sandstone boulders, all 200 tons of them, came from within Arkansas, many from the south-central Ozark Mountains. One of the garden's distinguishing features, the self-supporting Full Moon Bridge, was constructed by a local artisan—third-generation stonemason Bob Lowrey.

Robert Byers, associate executive director at Garvan, arrived in the early 1990s, when the elderly Mrs. Garvan was still visiting every day. His first job was to inventory all the plants on the site, including the original native specimens and those she had added. By the time he was finished, he had identified about 1,600 different plants.

The Asian plants sited here grow well in Arkansas's climate—and very quickly. As in many American Japanese-style gardens, they need to be continually pruned to preserve the carefully planned vistas. But perhaps it's fitting that this garden should have a little trouble with overzealous plants. Its lush acres developed from once deforested land serve as a testament to both the regenerative powers of nature and the potential of thoughtful garden design.

Typically, Japanese gardens in the United States bring in Japanese craftspeople to create structures, but here, a local stonemason was hired to create this unique bridge.

Japanese Home Gardens: Design and Layout

Asher Browne

You can take inspiration from the Japanese gardening tradition to create a serene and beautiful retreat of your own. Consider how the basic tenets can be applied to a small backyard, courtyard, rooftop garden, or other private space. As you have seen in earlier chapters, Japanese gardens are created to mirror nature, often in a distilled way. Whereas the typical Western garden tends to showcase geometric arrangements of colorful spring- and summer-blooming plants, Japanese gardens are designed to create views inspired by nature, like mountains, forests, and rocky coastlines.

Appreciating Small Spaces

The detail-oriented nature of the Japanese garden tradition offers small gardens an advantage over larger ones. In an intimate space, the viewer is more likely to notice high-quality stone and skillfully pruned trees, for example. Attention to other details like the type of the fence materials also really pays off.

You can use a similar approach in your own garden. Remember that seasonality is a key component. Like the natural world, a garden can be beautiful year-round, and a design that includes thoughtful hardscaping in harmony with smart plant choices can accomplish this. The composition of your garden should also reflect nature. Layouts should be asymmetrical, as should the individual garden elements—a path that meanders like a stream, a conifer pruned to appear windswept. Below and in the next chapters, you will see practical ways to accomplish these goals.

Consider Your Space and Aesthetics

Most likely, the garden space that you are designing will serve some kind of purpose. It might simply be as an outdoor "room" to spend time in, or it might have a more specific function, like an entrance or pathway. For example, you might have a small space that includes a path leading from a side door to the driveway or street. In Japan, these practical spaces, even if narrow or small, are often laid out to be aesthetically

The combination of thoughtful plant choices, tasteful rock arrangements, and an attractive enclosure make this small viewing garden very successful.

pleasant. When planning any functional garden, you will need to take into account necessary elements, like pathways and access points.

In some situations you might want to create a viewing garden—a sort of living painting intended to be seen but not entered. These are most often seen in public spaces like restaurants or hotels, but they are also appropriate for certain residential spaces, for example an enclosed courtyard of an apartment building. Since such a garden will not be occupied or walked through, there's no need for paths or stepping-stones other than perhaps for visual interest. The landscape may be seen from a window or glass door, and the main goal is to create the best view from all vantage points.

You will also want to think about your garden concept, the general feel or mood you want to produce. Will the garden be rustic, like a tea garden, and create the calming effect of a mountain path? Or will it be more stylized and formal, like a dry rock garden with pines that evokes a rocky coast?

Choose Major Elements

Once you have a general garden concept, its time to choose the major elements in your garden. For this, it's helpful to first understand the parts that make up the whole. A focal point is an element that visually anchors the garden. It could be a rock arrangement, a waterfall, a specimen tree, a stone ornament, or a water basin.

First decide what the focal point should be and where to locate it in relation to necessary functional elements. Japanese gardens are balanced but in an asymmetrical way, so the focal point is never in the dead center of a symmetrical arrangement. It is often placed toward the back and to one side, with other features set accordingly. The goal is to create a dynamic yet balanced composition that guides the viewer's eye from one element to another and back to the focal point. This flow creates a sense of calm. The composition of a small garden should not be complex, so make sure that the surrounding elements are a good match for the focal point. Here are some elements you might use to anchor your design.

Rock Arrangements

You can use boulders and smaller stones to evoke mountains, waterfalls, islands, rocky coastlines, and other natural features. As long as the arrangement is scaled to the size of the space, there are no restrictions; even small gardens in Japan make use of rocks. You can convey the beauty of stone simply and in a balanced way with an array of only three to five stones, or even one or two if the space is particularly tiny. The key is to select stones with good shape, color, and texture.

Water Basins

Many small gardens in Japan use a water basin as a focal point. This element, often found in tea gardens, tends to be a good fit proportionally and is a simple

A single, well-placed ornament, like a stone lantern (left), can add important visual impact. An array of stones with good shape and texture can be composed to great effect (right).

and practical way to include water. A basin may be a natural boulder with a depression carved into it or a more formal, designed shape carved out of granite. A pump may be used to circulate water through a spout, which adds sensory interest—trickling water sounds as lovely as it looks.

Stone Ornaments

Lanterns are the most common stone ornaments found in Japanese gardens, but sometimes structures like small pagodas are used. Ornaments can be used alone or with another feature and are usually assembled on-site, making them a good option when a rock arrangement or water basin is not possible due to limited access or weight restrictions. As when selecting boulders, choose high-quality materials for ornaments. You should also look for a tasteful design that isn't overly ornate.

Specimen Trees

A specimen tree can be a great focal point and have just as much impact as an ornament or rock. The success of this option depends upon the beauty of the tree and the skill with which it is pruned. In Japan, pines are a common choice, as are many varieties of Japanese maple. Many other small ornamental species could work too. The key is to find a specimen with good trunk character and bring out that character with skillful pruning over time. (Also see "Specimen Trees," page 81.)

A stepping-stone path (left) looks rustic and also slows one's pace. A smooth, flat path (right) looks sleek and allows a person to step confidently while looking into the distance.

Pathways

Pathways should not follow a straight line but rather be laid out at an angle or curve. This adds visual interest and allows for wide spaces for garden features and plantings. Keep the perspective of people walking through the garden in mind when planning the path. How will the view change as they proceed? The materials you choose will also affect the look and feel of the garden. Widely spaced, irregular stepping-stones, for instance, will give the space a more rustic appearance and cause visitors to walk slowly and with care, whereas a flat or gravel path will look sleek and allow people to walk more freely and look about the garden.

Enclosure

Integration of the house and garden is an important part of the Japanese tradition, and enclosure plays a crucial role in achieving this integration. For a room facing the garden, the garden's enclosure provides privacy from the outside world, as well as a sense of intimacy with the outdoor space. Visually, not only is the living space extended to the outer enclosure, but the garden is also pulled into the home. What better way to enhance the quality of our time indoors?

A garden may be enclosed by walls, fences, hedges, or mass plantings. There are advantages and disadvantages to each. Sometimes the most refined solution comes from combining two types of enclosure. Small urban gardens may already be partially

Fix Drainage Problems Earlier Rather than Later

Poor drainage is a common yet often overlooked concern with small gardens. This can be caused by runoff from roofs, poor grading within or outside the garden, a blocked drain, poor soil, or a combination of these factors. The standing water that collects as a result may damage structures. It can also breed pests and cause root rot, which can damage or even kill plants. Examine and test your site in the planning stages and make note of whether and where water collects and how long it takes to drain or soak into the soil.

Solutions Address problems now, not later. For a garden within a suburban yard, you can forestall drainage problems by making sure the soil is a healthy mix of loam and sand, with good structure. The ground should be graded to slope away from the house. If necessary, you can also install a channel, ideally obscured, for runoff.

In small urban gardens, you may need to make more effort to give water an escape. Look for existing drains or channels out of the garden and make sure they are in good repair, or install new ones. Then check that excess water can make its way to the drain, whether via a drainage pipe or by grading. If you are working with a roof garden, clean or repair gutters and ensure that they are adequate.

Well-draining, healthy soil is especially important for the well-being of the garden. Check the basic texture of the soil by sticking a shovel in the ground. Sandy soil is easy to dig; clayey soil is more likely to be dense and compacted; and rocky soil may be loose but hard to dig. It's also a good idea to have a soil sample assessed by your local cooperative extension service before any planting is done, and then add compost and other amendments to improve structure.

or fully enclosed by the walls of adjacent buildings, in which case screening, like fencing or climbing vines can be used to improve the aesthetics if necessary. (Also see "Screening Plants," page 84.)

Mindful Garden Planning

Don't build a garden that's too difficult for you to maintain. Make a careful assessment of your site before starting to design, and again before installation, to avoid costly mistakes. For example, if you install a tall hedge along the back of a garden plot that suddenly drops off, you will have no practical way to shear the back of the hedge. If you plant a specimen tree that requires labor-intensive pruning beyond your skill level, you'll need to budget for a professional to tend to it annually. Always plan and build with future maintenance in mind. (See "Maintaining Your Garden," page 92, to get a sense of what's in store.)

Plant Selection and Planting Scheme

Asher Browne

The best designs for Japanese gardens often involve simple solutions to complex problems. To get just the right effect, plantings must suit the site conditions, complement and balance the hardscaping, conform to your aesthetic style, include year-round seasonal interest, and fit within your budget and maintenance plan. The good news is that once you consider all these factors, you can usually arrive at the right plant choices by the process of elimination.

To compose a beautiful garden that mirrors a natural landscape in a balanced way, look for plants in a range of sizes and types. Each will serve a role in your design. Below are the traditional roles plants play in Japanese gardening, along with an array of suitable choices.

Specimen Trees

The main plant features of a Japanese garden are the specimen trees. These are considered the most elegant or refined trees, and they are not to be upstaged by other trees or shrubs. They are usually positioned in a way that showcases their beauty, and they are typically pruned to draw out certain features. Traditionally these features include a gracefully curved S-shaped trunk, cascading layers of horizontal branches, and enough space between branches to reveal the tree's trunk and branch structure. (Also see "Pruning Specimen Trees," page 93.)

Large pine trees are the classic specimen trees associated with Japanese gardens. They can make stunning choices for focal points, though it does take a lot of time to develop and prune them. There are other options that might be more practical in many home gardens, including a wide range of other conifers, broadleaf evergreens, and "light" specimens—deciduous trees, which are visually less heavy than evergreens. These may have a natural-looking form and tend to look pleasing right away. They also require less pruning.

Deciduous shrubs pruned in a naturalistic, loose style require less pruning than conifers and give a garden an informal, soft look, as does a high ratio of plants to rocks. Foliage also provides seasonal interest in the form of dramatic fall color.

Shaped shrubs lend a crisp feel to a garden, especially in combination with gravel and rock arrangements. Broadleaf evergreens are a typical choice.

Good Choices Traditional conifer species include Japanese black pine (*Pinus thunbergii*), Japanese white pine (*P. parviflora*), Austrian pine (*P. nigra*), and Scots pine (*P. sylvestris*). Pitch pine (*P. rigida*) is one of the few North American natives that would work in a Japanese garden.

Other suitable conifers include hinoki cypress (*Chamaecyparis obtusa*), yews (*Taxus* species), Chinese juniper (*Juniperus chinensis*), and cultivars such as the dwarf blue spruce (*Picea pungens* 'Montgomery') and Sargeant weeping hemlock (*Tsuga canadensis* 'Pendula'). Broadleaf evergreens that can handle winters include some hollies (*Ilex* species) and *Camellia* species.

Japanese maples (*Acer palmatum*) are among the most common light specimen trees in Japanese gardens. For small gardens, varieties that can be contained at a height of 12 feet or less work best, like cutleaf maple (*A. palmatum* var. *dissectum*). Dogwoods (*Cornus* species), Japanese snowbell (*Styrax japonicus*), stewartia (*Stewartia pseudocamellia*), and crepe-myrtles (*Lagerstroemia* species) also make good specimens. Native trees like serviceberry (*Amelanchier canadensis*), eastern redbud (*Cercis canadensis*), flowering dogwood (*Cornus florida*), and American hornbeam (*Carpinus caroliniana*) can also be used to great effect, as can native hawthorns (*Crataegus* species) and birches (*Betula* species).

Shaped Shrubs

In Japan, shaped shrubs are commonly used to add body to the garden composition. Placing them around boulders and at the base of trees can add dimension and prevent the landscape from feeling flat. Shaped shrubs also deliver a sense of crispness; that is, when the shrubs are sheared neatly, the garden feels somehow cleaner.

Good Choices Azaleas (*Rhododendron* species) are the most common choice in Japan, but Japanese holly (*Ilex crenata*), which looks a lot like a boxwood, is also used. Korean boxwood (*Buxus microphylla* var. *koreana*) is another fairly versatile and hardy choice. Inkberry (*Ilex glabra*) is a good native option, especially as a mass of shaped shrubs behind shorter plants.

Natural Shrubs, Large and Small

Shrubs that exhibit a looser, more natural look are used either in gardens that have a less formal look in general or in combination with shaped shrubs for a balanced composition. There are many great options, both broadleaf evergreen and deciduous.

Good Choices Small broadleaf evergreen shrubs include Japanese andromeda (*Pieris japonica*), Japanese and native *Rhododendron* varieties, Japanese aucuba (*Aucuba japonica*), camellias, Japanese skimmia (*Skimmia japonica*), and native mountain laurel (*Kalmia latifolia*). Somewhat larger broadleaf evergreens include rhododendrons,

Azaleas are often sheared into domed shapes, but they can also be allowed to grow in a looser, more natural-looking style, which also allows more flowers to bloom in the spring.

Photinia species, heavenly bamboo (*Nandina domestica*), and hollies such as inkberry (*Ilex glabra*) and longstalk holly (*I. pedunculosa*). Many varieties of evergreen viburnums can also work.

Small deciduous shrubs like Japanese beautyberry (*Callicarpa japonica*), *Enkianthus* species, flowering quinces (*Chaenomeles* species), and deciduous azaleas also make good plants for small Japanese gardens. Native options include oakleaf hydrangea (*Hydrangea quercifolia*) and dwarf fothergilla (*Fothergilla gardenii*).

Screening Plants

Screening plants are trees or large shrubs—usually evergreen—placed to block an unwanted view that could disrupt the overall effect or scale of the garden. Even if that view cannot be completely hidden, it can at least be softened by thoughtful plantings. Deciduous plants may work if screening during the winter is not important. Screening plants also help enclose the garden.

Good Choices Various types of holly, including North American varieties and upright Japanese holly (*Ilex crenata*), arborvitae (*Thuja* species), hinoki cypress (*Chamaecyparis* species), *Photinia* species, and *Osmanthus* species can all work as screening. If there's enough space, screening plants can also be massed together in a staggered line or in layers rather than a dense hedge. Long-stalk holly (*I. pedunculosa*), leatherleaf viburnum (*Viburnum rhytidophyllum*), andromeda (*Pieris* species), camellias, and *Rhododendron* species would make good choices for this. If screening in the winter isn't necessary, then deciduous viburnums make good massed screen plantings.

Groundcovers

The garden cannot consist entirely of shrubs and trees. The way the open areas are laid out and planted has a great deal to do with creating a dynamic composition. There are a number of low-growing groundcovers that can be used.

Good Choices Most people associate moss with Japanese gardens, and it makes a stunning groundcover when it is successful. Keep in mind, however, that moss can be difficult to establish—and difficult to maintain. It must be weeded and watered more often than most homeowners expect. A common alternative in Japan is dwarf mondo grass (*Ophiopogon japonicus* 'Nanus'). Also consider Irish moss (*Chondrus crispus*), short *Sedum* varieties, *Vinca* and *Pachysandra* species, and turf grasses. Taller plants like lily-turf (*Liriope* species) and hakone grass (*Hakonechloa macra*) also work well.

Gravel is a good non-plant alternative for open areas and is often used instead of or in combination with groundcover plants. It can be an excellent choice in a small garden for both aesthetic and functional reasons, though it does require regular weeding and debris removal.

Clockwise from top left: Sasanqua camellia (*Camellia sasanqua* 'Autumn Sunrise'),
Japanese beautyberry (*Callicarpa japonica*), Yodogawa azalea (*Rhododendron yedoense*),
white enkianthus (*Enkianthus perulatus* 'J.l. Pennock'), Japanese maple (*Acer palmatum*),
Japanese pieris (*Pieris japonica* 'Dorothy Wyckoff').

Moss is a classic groundcover, though it requires a lot of maintenance, including frequent weeding and watering. *Sedum* varieties and turf can be used to create a similar effect.

Creating a Good Balance

A balanced design is crucial for the success of a Japanese-inspired garden. Here are a few guidelines to keep in mind.

Deciduous to Evergreen Ratio

Not only do deciduous plants lose their leaves in the winter, they also have a different feel during the warm months. Evergreens, including broadleaf species, tend to look denser and heavier, while deciduous plants often seem lighter. In Japan, gardens are often planted with a higher ratio of evergreens to deciduous plants compared with those in the United States. Evergreens make for a greener garden through the winter months and can also serve as a backdrop for the changing features of the deciduous plants. There is no exact guideline, but traditional Japanese plantings usually have five evergreens to every two to three deciduous plants.

Rock to Plant Ratio

A design with more stone than plants will give your garden an austere and formal feel. More plants will give it a softer, more natural look. Think of this as a spectrum, with all rocks on one end, and all plants on the other. The perfect balance depends on the effect you want, but it's likely somewhere in the middle. Include enough stone for impact and form, but also enough plantings to soften and balance it out.

Assessing Site Conditions

Plants must be sited correctly to stay healthy and beautiful. A specimen pine, for example, cannot go just anywhere. Plant it in a shady location, and even if it lives, it will not thrive. Likewise, if you put it on a site with poor drainage, it will eventually develop root rot. Plant selection is not an exact science, but picking the most appropriate plants is easier when you know the site conditions beforehand.

Full Sun, Full Shade, or Somewhere in Between

Assessing the light conditions is a good first step. Ideally, Japanese gardens are placed near homes or other structures. Unfortunately, in urban and some suburban settings, this usually means the garden will be in partial or full shade, so you'll need to choose plants that tolerate partial or full shade. Even if you have a sunny site, remember that certain specimen trees, if not trimmed annually, will eventually shade out the rest of a small garden. In this case, select a tree that does well in sun, but choose shrubs and other plants that will thrive in partial to full shade.

Soil Quality

A plant's health depends as much on what happens below the soil line as what happens above it. Put a shovel into the ground to get a rough idea of what the soil is like. Is the soil sandy, heavy clay, or, like most, somewhere in between? It's always worthwhile to have the soil tested by a cooperative extension service. It could have

Why Choose Native Plants?

The plants in your Japanese garden don't necessarily have to be Japanese species. The most admired Japanese-style public gardens in the United States feature a mix of North American and Asian plants, and yours should too. You could even create an entirely native garden using Japanese gardening tenets, design elements, and pruning techniques.

Native plants have evolved to handle local soils and seasonal variations in rainfall and temperature, so they sometimes require less maintenance. They are also good ecological choices—natives are very unlikely to become invasive, and they provide habitat and resources for native birds, beneficial insects, and other wildlife. Be sure to consider some of the North American native plant options listed in this chapter, like mountain laurel (*Kalmia latifolia*), above, for your garden.

too much or too little of certain nutrients, or it might be too acidic or too alkaline. If necessary, amending the soil can usually wait until after the hardscaping is done, but it's still best to address it early in the garden-building process, before plants are placed.

Drainage

Bad drainage usually stems from one or more of three things: poor soil, like heavy clay, that doesn't allow water to seep through it; an improperly pitched surface that fails to allow excess rainwater to run off; or lack of a drain or other route for excess water to drain. Address these issues before you start planting. Topsoil can be amended or changed. The ground can be regraded to carry runoff away. A drain or other watercourse can be installed to take water out of the garden. This should be planned and installed during the hardscaping phase. (Also see "Fix Drainage Problems Earlier Rather than Later," page 79.)

Wind Conditions

Wind can dry out a site at any time of year, and in the winter a biting wind can severely burn the foliage of evergreen plants. This is particularly true for rooftop or terrace gardens on higher floors. Is your site, or part of it, exposed to strong winds? If so, consider putting up a fence to help protect plantings, or select plants that tolerate a windy situation.

The plants in this Japanese-style rooftop garden are sheltered from the wind by an adjacent wall, a fence, and a small teahouse.

Choosing a Planting Scheme

Gardens look best when the palette of plants is limited and they are sited with a clear, strong effect in mind. This is particularly true in a small garden, since there just is not enough space to include many kinds of different plants. Use your site assessment and aesthetic goals to narrow your plant choices to those that will both thrive and convey simplicity and refinement.

Site Conditions

When you take your site conditions into account at the outset, you will reduce the list of plant possibilities quite a bit. The size of the space is a major factor; for example, if your garden is small, there may only be enough room for one tree. And as mentioned above, that tree could eventually reduce the amount of sunlight available to other plants. If the site is already somewhat shady, sun-loving species should be crossed off the list.

Aesthetics

Once you know what your site conditions will allow, the garden concept guides the rest of the process. If your space is to be formal and stylized, you might choose pine trees with stunning form, shaped shrubs like azaleas or boxwood, and gravel in the open areas. If your goal is a rustic look, you might choose more naturalistic shrubs and trees—perhaps a small Japanese maple and andromeda—to accompany stepping-stones and a water basin.

Fine-Tuning over Time

Even the best-researched planting schemes will inevitably have a small number of failures—plants that just do not work out. Be prepared to try plant alternatives that still convey your desired effect. Before replacing plants, use the opportunity to reassess the site. The general conditions of sunlight, water, and wind may not have changed since you planned the garden, but the process of creating it may have introduced a change, perhaps a new fence, irrigation system, or drainage course that creates a slightly different environment.

It is a mistake to consider the initial garden concept so sacred that it can never be altered. If over the years a better solution or slight refinement can be made that improves the garden, then make it. There are many famous gardens in Japan that have been refined in this way over the years, and they are the better for it.

Maintenance and Pruning

Asher Browne

In Japan, they say it takes ten years for a garden to become complete. Time is needed for trees, shrubs, groundcovers, and other plants to fill in. Shaping trees and shrubs into more finished forms also takes years. When planning your own Japanese garden, be aware of the specialized maintenance that may be involved, in particular, pruning.

Care and Development

Japanese gardens require both routine care and ongoing development. You will need to devote some time to typical tasks like cleaning, weeding, fertilizing, watering, and pest and disease control on a regular basis. Hardscaping elements also require some work. Over time, you will need to repair any damage due to frost heave, rot, and wear and tear.

The development of a Japanese garden is a long-term process. The word "maintenance" implies that a garden may be kept in a state of stasis, but the truth is that trees and shrubs are living things that are always changing. In the Japanese tradition, much more so than in a typical Western garden, pruning is used over time to control the size of trees and shrubs as well as to create more beautiful forms. Whether you have enough pruning expertise to tend to your garden yourself or plan to hire a professional, it will help to review the goals and techniques involved in pruning various types of trees and shrubs.

Pruning Basics

Initially, a pruner works to develop the form of a tree or shrub. This process takes time, but eventually the form will seem just right, and then the focus will shift to maintaining that form. As trees and shrubs mature, those that continue to push and expand their limits can often be judiciously shaped and pruned to limit growth. There are also more aggressive Japanese pruning techniques for maintaining form over long periods of time, but the best strategy for keeping a home garden balanced is to choose appropriate plants and site them carefully in the first place. (See "Plant Selection and Planning Scheme," page 80.)

In the Japanese tradition, trees and shrubs, especially conifers, are pruned regularly by an expert to develop their characteristic shapes over time.

Maintaining Your Garden: What to Expect

Japanese-style gardens are not generally low maintenance; in fact, they often require more care and attention than typical Western-style landscaping. A thorough maintenance plan is key to keeping your garden healthy and beautiful year-round.

Pruning of trees and shrubs

This task requires the most skill and expertise and therefore may be the one thing for which you will hire a professional, even if you are an avid gardener. Specimen plants will require one or two pruning sessions a year. Other trees and shrubs will benefit from one major pruning annually and a touch-up trim in between.

Regular fertilizing, watering, and mulching

Don't forget to allow time for these all-important tasks. Fertilize and mulch in the spring and fall, and water sufficiently year-round.

Spring and fall cleanup

Remove fallen leaves and debris at the beginning of the season and just before winter. Expect to do additional cleanup after pruning and as needed when plants drop leaves, pinecones, fruit, and dead twigs.

Care for groundcovers and other perennials, large and small

Perennials often require work like deadheading or cutting back at specific times, so be sure to research the plants you have chosen. For example, dwarf bamboo should be left through the winter to provide seasonal interest and then trimmed in spring to encourage new growth.

Weeding

Keep your garden religiously weeded so it will look well groomed and crisp. If you fail to do so, it will look messy, no matter how well you maintain everything else.

Care for decorative gravel

Gravel features require regular weeding. Debris like fallen leaves will also need to be removed from them often.

Repair of paths

Over time, you may need to reset stepping-stones that have shifted due to frost heave. Paths set with stone dust may need to be refreshed with dust periodically.

Drain maintenance

Make sure drains and runoff pathways are functioning properly. Check and clear drains at least once a year and whenever there's been a significant storm. Scrape and regrade runoff pathways as needed.

Pruning Specimen Trees

Specimen plantings—trees and shrubs meant as focal points in the garden—can end up looking wildly different depending on their type, age, character, and the pruner's choices, but they share a few basic characteristics. All specimen trees have a layered canopy of branches and a visible trunk. They are smaller on the top and wider at the bottom, even those with a windswept form. Usually their tops are slightly rounded.

The pruner encourages branches to grow horizontally and controls their length so that they are progressively shorter as they get closer to the top. This creates a more stable-looking form. The pruner also thins the foliage to allow sunlight and air to reach the bottom branches and thins the interior foliage and smaller branches to allow space between the main branches and create alternating layers. The rounded top can be achieved by removing the tip of the central trunk when the tree has reached its desired height. Then, with years of skillful pruning, the top can be developed into a more finished, rounded shape.

Some specimen trees will have more space between the horizontal branches than others. For example, a 15-foot-tall Japanese red pine (*Pinus densiflora*) may be pruned more to show off the attractive trunk, whereas a 6-foot-tall cutleaf Japanese maple (*Acer palmatum* 'Dissectum') would have more subtle spacing since it has a canopy of weeping foliage.

This Japanese black pine has been shaped over many years by pruning. Branches were judiciously removed to reveal its trunk and create a windswept look.

A branch layer will not necessarily consist of a single branch. Sometimes multiple branches contribute to form one layer. Layers should be staggered throughout the canopy to avoid the appearance of rings around the tree. By creating such branch structure, and by thinning evenly throughout, you will reveal the trunk. A tree's unique character seems to come alive when its trunk is visible through the canopy of branch layers, especially if it exhibits ornamental bark or windswept form. When choosing specimens at the nursery, look closely at the trunk and main branches to make sure there is potential to develop this character.

Pines and other conifers are typically pruned in late September or October. The tree is first thinned out, and the oldest pine needles may be removed. These old pine needles would eventually fall anyway, and removing them gives the tree a lighter look. Doing so also lets more sunlight and air reach the smaller buds, a key to maintaining good form over time. Ample small buds are then ready to replace the larger ones. Candling is a secondary technique. This consists of trimming off part of the new growth (called candles) in the spring, usually the end of May or June. Ideally, this limits new growth and gives the pruner more choices when it is time to thin out branches in the fall.

Deciduous and broadleaf evergreen specimen trees are also pruned for a layered canopy, but they usually retain a more natural look than conifers. There is less space between branches, and the overall form may appear lighter and looser. The trunk and branch structure may be less visible, but can still be glimpsed through the foliage.

Deciduous trees, like these cutleaf Japanese maples, retain a looser look than conifers when pruned, but their trunk and branch structure is still revealed.

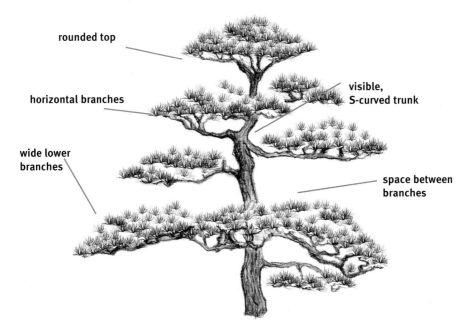

rounded top

horizontal branches

wide lower branches

visible, S-curved trunk

space between branches

A well-pruned specimen tree has a windswept form with several key characteristics. Achieving such a look requires years of expert pruning.

Deciduous trees like maples can be pruned any time of year, but in general, shaping cuts are made in late winter, when the structure of the tree is visible. Thinning is best done in summer, after new growth hardens off. This allows you to create a more finished look in one pruning session with only minor touch-ups needed. Broadleaf evergreens can also be pruned at any time of year, but doing so in late winter or early spring will maximize flower and berry production.

Tips for Pruning Specimen Trees

Have Patience

Don't overprune or otherwise rush the process of shaping a specimen tree. In an attempt to uncover the tree's character and create a more dynamic form, an inexperienced pruner may cut out too many main branches, leaving large gaps and an overexposed trunk. Not only does this look unrefined, it could also be unhealthy for the tree. Achieving a graceful finished form takes time—several years or more. In Japan, most high-quality trees are decades in the making, if not centuries. Pruning too much in a single year will only delay your overall goal of creating a beautiful one-of-a-kind specimen.

Hide Pruning Cuts

Good pruning doesn't draw attention to itself. After the job is done, the tree should look thinned out and lighter, but there shouldn't be hundreds of visible pruning cuts all over the tree. This is important with all specimens, but pruning cuts can look especially harsh with certain conifers and deciduous trees that are supposed to look natural. During yearly pruning, first remove the larger branches and do necessary structural pruning, then thin out the canopy, masking as many pruning cuts as possible. This may entail trimming branches near the base of a larger branch, leaving the foliage at the tips of that larger branch untouched. This has a much softer overall appearance and is a reason to avoid tipping branches on certain trees. Pruning lightly and frequently also helps.

Natural-Looking Shrubs

Most shrubs are pruned in the same way as natural-looking specimen trees but don't take as much attention. Whether they are deciduous or broadleaf evergreen, large or small, the basic concept is still to encourage a strong and layered branch structure, with less emphasis on horizontal layering. As with trees, shrubs should be thinned for a lighter look.

Shaped Shrubs

Massed shrubs or single dome-shaped shrubs like azaleas or boxwoods are usually trimmed for shape with hand pruners or hedge shears once in early summer and then lightly at least once or twice later in the summer and early fall. A looser look can be achieved with hand snips. Since the act of shearing will create a dense top layer, it is wise to thin out that top layer periodically to allow sun to penetrate to the interior.

Hedges and Massed Plantings

Unless hedges are exceedingly long or tall, they can also be trimmed with hand shears. Tall hedges can be trimmed with power shears. Trim the sides first to make it easier to shear the top in a level line. Another common technique is to shear the sides of the hedge starting on the left side and moving toward the right side. When the shears are used correctly, the tip of the blades point to the right and "throw" the clippings downward. Going from right to left would toss the clippings into the air and possibly into the hedge, making for more cleanup.

Groupings of small trees or large shrubs should be pruned for shape in a similar way as natural-looking shrubs. Plants used for screening may be kept thicker to provide privacy.

Shaped shrubs like boxwoods are usually sheared by hand. This should be done thoroughly in early summer and then again lightly to touch up later in the summer or early fall.

Hiring a Professional Pruner

Most Japanese-style gardens will require specialized pruning to develop and maintain trees and shrubs, and most home gardeners will want to enlist the help of an expert for this. Look for someone who has expertise and training in aesthetic pruning. If you have a lot of conifers, plan on having the pruner come at least once a year, ideally twice—in the spring and in the fall if possible.

Specimens will require the most attention, so they should be made the highest priority, but other trees and shrubs will also benefit from expert shaping too. Your pruner should also be able to give you specific advice on how to maintain your plants between visits.

Tool Kit for a Japanese Garden

Brian Funk

It's worth investing in Japanese-made tools and gear to care for your garden. Japanese craftsmanship is superior, perhaps because garden-blade making in Japan grew out of the sword-making tradition. Whatever the reason, today's Japanese tools tend to be more ergonomic and lightweight than typical garden tools, and they are generally made from higher-quality steel. They are efficient and precise, don't degrade quickly due to wear and tear, and just seem more enjoyable to use. Many are specialized for a particular task, allowing you to choose just the right tool for the job at hand. A set including tools like those described here would cover most of the work you'd do in a residential garden.

Hori hori

One of the great all-purpose gardening tools, a hori hori is a combination trowel and soil knife that can be used for cultivating, digging, weeding, and planting. They are typically about a foot long with a seven-inch blade.

Bonsai Scissors

These classically designed pruners can be used for detail work on smaller branches and for removing new growth on pines (candling). When you thin and shape your trees and shrubs between professional visits, you can use these for precision cuts that are too fine for larger hand pruners. It's worth getting a leather holster or sheath so you can carry them safely and conveniently.

Loppers

Long-handled loppers like these are good for cutting medium-sized branches (thicker than your thumb, but less than an inch or so in diameter). They have better reach than hand pruners and are handy for reaching the interior of a shrub or small tree.

Pocket Saw

Use this small foldable saw to remove branches that are too thick for loppers (over one inch in diameter). It's portable and can be carried fairly easily in your pocket while you climb a ladder or a tree. (However, don't climb trees to prune unless you have the training and expertise to do so.) Most have tricut blades which cut easier and faster than typical blades do. Gomboy and Gomtaru are two good-quality brands.

Hedge Shears

These shears are for general-purpose trimming and can be used to create the gentle curves in Japanese-style massed hedges (*okarikomi*) or domed-shape shrubs (*tamamono*).

Hoe and Sickle

Both of these tools can be used for weeding. The hoe (left) is more multipurpose and can be used as a cultivator or a hand hoe for breaking up compacted soil and leveling small areas. The sickle (right) is more specialized for weeding and is excellent for cutting weed roots.

Bamboo Saw

If you are growing bamboo, you'll need this saw for cutting it while it's green. The fine-toothed blade cuts without splintering or ripping plant fibers. It can also be used for carpentry.

Jikatabi

Split-toed, soft-soled shoes or boots give you more sensitivity and a better grip than traditional boots while working in the garden. They also have a lighter impact if you need to walk over mossy patches or planted areas, and they're easier on bark if you need to climb a tree.

Glossary
Marc Peter Keane

chanoyu Tea ceremony. Literally, "hot water for tea," the term refers to the culture of holding subdued artistic gatherings, usually for a small number of guests, at which powdered tea (*matcha*) is served.

daimyo Feudal lord. Until 1871, when the feudal system ended, each daimyo controlled vast landholdings, where he had a castle and estate; he also maintained one or more residences in the capital city of Edo. Extensive gardens were often developed on these properties. See *kaiyushiki-teien*.

engetsukyo Literally, "full moon bridge." The half-barrel shape of this style of bridge is reflected in the water below it to form a complete circle that evokes a full moon. Chinese in origin, these bridges were used in Japanese stroll gardens to create the exotic atmosphere of ancient China.

kaiyushiki-teien Stroll garden. The term refers to gardens built on the estates of feudal lords (see *daimyo*) and some aristocratic families. Typically these gardens were large and featured a central lake. Meandering paths were created to circumambulate the lake, allowing strolling visitors to take in the changing views.

karesansui Dry landscape garden. Written with three characters denoting "dry," "mountain," and "water," karesansui refers to gardens that represent the natural landscape through the placement of boulders and smaller stones or pebbles. Instead of actual water, karesansui gardens employ gravel raked into patterns to mimic ocean waves or carefully placed palm-sized stones to evoke running water.

kisei Inherent force or energy. Each object placed in a garden, such as a stone or tree, has an inherent force or energy that needs to be understood and respected by the gardener who positions it. The gardener perceives this force through the stone or tree's shape and character. In the ancient gardening text the *Sakuteiki*, this was expressed as "following the request" of the object.

ma Interstitial space. The white area left unpainted in an ink landscape painting or in a work of calligraphy, the periods of silence in bamboo flute music, the simplicity of "empty" rooms in Japanese architecture, and the open spaces in garden design are all referred to as ma.

niwaki Garden trees. The term refers to a select group of trees particularly suited for use in the garden, including Japanese black pine, Japanese red pine, Japanese maple, Japanese stewartia, camellia, and Japanese apricot. In North America, niwaki can also refer to the style in which Japanese garden trees are traditionally pruned.

okarikomi Large-scale topiary: *Karikomi* means "clipped," and the prefix *o* means "large." This term refers to shrubbery that has been tightly sheared, usually to resemble a landscape scene, such as a flowing mountain range. Karikomi are most commonly made using Satsuki azaleas, but other densely leafed evergreen shrubs can also be employed.

pagoda Buddhist tower. In Japanese temple architecture, a pagoda is typically a wooden tower with five or seven roofs built with highly complex joinery, especially evident in the roof joists. The pagoda holds a Buddhist relic within and is thus the landmark structure of a Buddhist temple. In Japanese gardens, stone pagodas, sculpted granite versions that mimic wooden ones, are more often used.

roji Tea garden. First developed in the 16th century as an entry path to a teahouse, the design of the tea garden has influenced almost all Japanese gardens that developed thereafter. Roji built on large properties may have an outer and inner section and contain any of the following: an outer entry gate (*sotomon*) that separates the garden from the street; stepping-stone paths leading through the roji; a roofed waiting bench where guests can wait to be greeted; a middle gate (*chumon*) that marks the passage from outer to inner garden; a water basin (*tsukubai*) at which guests ritually cleanse themselves; and woodland evergreen plantings, including moss as a groundcover.

shiki Four seasons. Because the central region of Japan, where much of ancient Japanese culture developed, has four distinct seasons, clear seasonal motifs are incorporated in garden design as well as in painting, poetry, and other creative expression.

Shinto The native religion of Japan, literally, "way of the gods." The Shinto religion considers select places in nature and elements of the natural world to be sacred, including certain large boulders, ancient trees, and waterfalls. The design and development of the Japanese garden was influenced by this sensitivity toward, and appreciation for, the natural world.

sukiya Teahouse architecture. A refined form of architecture that began with the design of teahouses in the 16th century and has since become the basic template for elegant residences in general. Sukiya architectural features are understated and natural and include elements such as exposed posts and beams in their natural rounded form, lightweight roofs made of cedar or copper shingles, clay plaster walls, tatami mats for flooring, multilayer paper interior doors, and single-layer paper doors on the exterior. Enclosed gardens are placed immediately adjacent to the home so that the doors may be kept open, integrating the indoor space and the natural world.

tamamono Literally, "round thing." This pruning term refers to densely leafed shrubs such as azaleas that have been pruned into single, ball-like shapes, and also to taller trees that have been pruned with a series of ball-like shapes on each ascending branch.

teien Garden. Comprised of two kanji (written characters), both of which mean "garden" individually, *teien* is commonly used in formal situations—especially in writing. The first part, *tei*, can also be pronounced *niwa*, the word most garden owners use to refer to their own gardens. The second part, *en*, is often found as a suffix in names of famous gardens such as Kenrokuen or Korakuen.

tsuboniwa Courtyard garden. The use of the term *tsubo* for this type of small garden built in a space between buildings dates from the Heian period (794–1185), when they were common in aristocratic homes. From the late Edo period (1600–1868) on, merchants and artisans often included tsubo gardens in their urban townhouses; today they can be found in many modern buildings as well.

tsukubai Water basin arrangement. A stone water basin that sits within a roughly circular arrangement of stones is referred to as a *tsukubai*, literally, "crouching-down place." In a tea garden, a water basin is situated to allow guests to cleanse their hands and mouth before the tea ceremony.

wabisabi The aesthetic of natural simplicity. In tea ceremony culture, the term refers to objects that are understated, have an elegant patina of age, are somehow imperfect, commonplace in origin, and appear artless or natural. This can include an irregularly handmade ceramic tea bowl, a flower arrangement made with just a few stems of seasonal plants, a flower vase made from a single piece of bamboo, or a garden with no showy flowers or ornate rocks that evokes the feeling of a forest walk (see *roji*).

yatsuhashi Zigzag plank bridge. Literally, "eight bridges," the word *yatsuhashi* originated in the ninth-century *Tales of Ise* in reference to a place where the Azuma River branches into eight streams with a bridge crossing each. The location is also famous for the irises that grow there. The classic yatsuhashi in a garden is a simple plank bridge laid out in a zigzag fashion, built over shallow water in which Japanese water irises grow.

yukimigata-doro Snow-viewing lantern. This style of stone lantern has four supportive legs and a wide circular or hexagonal roof that protects the lamp inside from being extinguished by precipitation. In winter, it collects an attractive covering of snow.

zokinoniwa Natural forest garden. The term *zoki* means "miscellaneous trees" and refers to species not traditional to Japanese gardens (see *niwaki*). A relatively modern gardening style that uses primarily young deciduous trees in clusters to create the feeling of a mountain forest, it includes trees such as konara oak, Japanese snowbell, sawthorn oak, and birches.

For More Information

FURTHER READING

Japanese Garden Design
Marc Peter Keane
Tuttle, 1996

Japanese Gardens
Günter Nitschke
Taschen, 1999

The Japanese Tea Garden
Marc Peter Keane
Stone Bridge, 2009

A Japanese Touch for Your Garden
Kiyoshi Seike
Kodansha, 1993

A Japanese Touch for Your Home
Koji Yagi
Kodansha, 1982

Mirei Shigemori: Modernizing the Japanese Garden
Christian Tschumi
Stone Bridge, 2005

Quiet Beauty: The Japanese Gardens of North America
Kendall H. Brown
Tuttle, 2013

Sakuteiki: A Modern Translation of Japan's Gardening Classic
Jiro Takei and Marc P. Keane
Tuttle, 2001

Secret Teachings in the Art of Japanese Gardens
David Slawson
Kodansha, 1987

Sukiya Living Magazine
Douglas M. Roth, publisher
www.rothteien.com

Themes in the History of Japanese Garden Art
Wybe Kuitert
University of Hawaii Press, 2002

TOOLS

A.M. Leonard
amleo.com

Hida Tool
hidatool.com

Niwaki
www.niwaki.com

ORNAMENTS

Schneible Fine Arts
schneiblefinearts.com

PLANTS

Forestfarm at Pacifica
forestfarm.com

Shin-Boku
shin-bokunursery.com

Tips for Planning Guided Tours

Elizabeth Peters

Visitors to Japanese gardens are often immediately drawn in, and they usually perceive that the design is distinct from that of other types of gardens. Guiding a small group of visitors through the garden in discussion can help them form a deeper understanding and appreciation of this tradition, which is why many gardens have staff or trained volunteers to offer interpretation.

If you are involved in planning such tours, learn about the history of your garden, its plants, and its significant features before you begin. Then plan a route in which you discuss particular elements or engage in conversations like those suggested below. A smaller group makes it much easier to carry on a conversation, and is less likely to disrupt the garden's tranquility, so limit the tour size when possible. As you plan, consider the tour's pace and potential seating along the route. A tour of 30 minutes is generally long enough to present the garden without tiring people. You can also design variations of your tour for each season or tailor it for different audiences.

Introduce your garden.

Welcome visitors, mention a highlight or two, and explain how long the tour will be and what the terrain is like. Then introduce the principles of Japanese garden design, and describe your particular garden's history, style, and major elements. Let visitors know about any special activities or events that take place in the garden, and cover rules and garden etiquette.

Conversation starters: *What comes to mind when you think about Japan? What do you know about Japanese gardens? Has anyone visited this garden before, maybe in another season or in years past? How does this garden make you feel?*

Encourage visitors to use their senses.

Ask people to pay attention to what they see, hear, smell, and feel as they walk through the space. Point out ways in which the garden's design fosters particular experiences. Perhaps the texture of the path affects the sound of footsteps or encourages a slower pace. Or maybe a twist in the path hides a dramatic vista before revealing it at a particular point farther along. Or maybe there is a rushing waterfall or gurgling stream that adds sound to the garden.

Conversation starters: *What do you see? What do you hear? What do you smell? Is your mood different in different parts of this garden? What choices did the garden's designer make that set the stage for these experiences?*

Point out the changing landscape.

Japanese gardens are often designed to present a sequence of composed views. A simple way to demonstrate this is to carry a small, empty picture frame and let participants take turns looking at various scenes through it. You may wish to discuss design elements such as asymmetry, balance, color, and movement, or select a spot where visitors can sketch what they see.

Conversation starters: *What do you see in the background/middle ground/foreground? What is changing and what is still? What other contrasts do you see? How did the garden's designer encourage you to notice this particular view?*

Remind participants of the intention behind the design.

Visitors sometimes overlook the extensive horticultural work that goes into creating natural-seeming scenes. Stop by a particular plant and talk about why it was selected for its specific location and how it is cared for. You might include topics like pruning techniques or the role of native plants in this discussion. You can also describe some of the structures or ornaments incorporated into the design.

Conversation starters: *What man-made structures do you see? How do they relate to the natural elements? Do you see any plants that you recognize? What kinds of things do people do in this garden?*

Help the group envision the changes that happen over time.

All gardens look different through the seasons and over the years. Have the group imagine how the garden's designer anticipated this. Describe some of the seasonal highlights you've seen, such as spring blossoms, fall foliage, or the snow covering on particular ornaments. Or select a mature tree and describe what it might have looked like years ago when it was first planted.

Conversation starters: *How would this view look in each season? What do you think this garden looked like when it first opened? How has the city around it changed since then? How might the garden appear 50 or 100 years in the future? Do you think the designer expected the plants to grow this way?*

Play a game.

A great way to encourage visitors, especially children, to connect with the environment is to conduct a scavenger hunt or play a similar game. Pick a theme, such as wildlife, water features, leaf shapes, or rock types, and have your group look for examples. (Be sure to discourage them from picking live plants or moving objects.) You can prepare a printed checklist or simply have group members call out their discoveries. Or have them "collect" items by taking photos or making sketches of them.

Conversation starters: *How many different shades of green do you see? Why do you think animals are attracted to this garden? Do you think these rocks were here when the garden was built, or were they placed here?*

Encourage further exploration.

At the conclusion of the tour, offer a brief wrap-up before suggesting that visitors continue exploring on their own. Recommend particular points of interest and resources for further study. Encourage the group members to return to the garden in other seasons or to participate in upcoming activities or events.

Conversation starters: *How did you feel while we were walking through the garden? Did any of your ideas about this place change during our tour? What do you hope to see next time you visit?*

Notable Japanese-Style Gardens in North America

There are more than 300 Japanese-style gardens in North America that are open to the public (most by admission). Below are some of the most highly regarded ones.

S = Stroll   **H** = House or Teahouse   **K** = Karesansui

		S	H	K
Amherst College – Yushien	Amherst, MA			
Anderson Japanese Gardens	Rockford, IL	•	•	•
Asticou Azalea Garden	Northeast Harbor, ME	•		•
Bloedel Reserve – Japanese Garden	Bainbridge Island, WA	•	•	•
Brooklyn Botanic Garden – Japanese Hill-and-Pond Garden	Brooklyn, NY	•		
Carleton College – Garden of Quiet Listening	Northfield, MN	•	•	•
Chicago Botanic Garden – Sansho En	Glencoe, IL	•	•	•
Cheekwood – Japanese Garden	Nashville, TN	•		•
Como Park Conservatory – Ordway Japanese Garden	St. Paul, MC	•		
Denver Botanic Gardens – Japanese Garden	Denver, CO	•	•	
Fort Worth Botanic Garden – Japanese Garden	Fort Worth, TX	•	•	•
Garvan Woodland Gardens – Garden of the Pine Wind	Hot Springs, AK	•		
Hakone	Saratoga, CA	•	•	•
The Huntington – Japanese Garden	San Marino, CA	•	•	•
Japanese Friendship Garden of Phoenix	Phoenix, AZ	•	•	
Japanese Friendship Garden	San Diego, CA	•	•	•
Golden Gate Park – Japanese Tea Garden	San Francisco, CA	•	•	
Maymont – Japanese Garden	Richmond, VA	•		
Minnesota Landscape Arboretum – Seisui Tei	Chaska, MN			
Missouri Botanical Garden – Sewa-en	St. Louis, MO	•	•	
Montreal Botanical Garden	Montreal, QC	•		•
Morikami Museum and Japanese Gardens	Delray Beach, FL	•	•	•
Museum of Fine Arts, Boston	Boston, MA		•	
Nikka Yuko Japanese Garden	Lethbridge, AB	•	•	•
Manito Park – Nishinomiya Garden	Spokane, WA	•		
Portland Japanese Garden	Portland, OR	•	•	•
San Mateo Central Park – Japanese Tea Garden	San Mateo, CA	•	•	
Seattle Japanese Garden	Seattle, WA	•	•	
Shofuso Japanese House and Garden	Philadelphia, PA	•	•	
Donald C. Tillman Water Reclamation Plant – Suiho En	Van Nuys, CA	•		•
Wesleyan University – Shoyoan Teien	Middletown, CT		•	
University of British Columbia – Nitobe Memorial Garden	Vancouver, BC	•	•	

Contributors

Asher Browne specializes in the design, construction and maintenance of Japanese gardens, including aesthetic pruning. He spent eight years in Japan, four of them training at garden companies in Kyoto. His website is www.asherbrowne.com.

Brian Funk is the curator of the Japanese Hill-and-Pond Garden at Brooklyn Botanic Garden. He has 35 years of experience as a landscape designer, garden builder, and aesthetic pruner. He studied gardening in Japan and is an avid bonsai and ikebana enthusiast. He also contributes to *Sukiya Living Magazine*.

Marc Peter Keane is a garden designer, educator, and author. Having lived in Kyoto for nearly 20 years, his garden design work is deeply influenced by the aesthetics and culture of Japan. His website is www.mpkeane.com.

Hoishi Kurisu is president and principal designer of Kurisu International, which he founded in 1972. He served as landscape director at the Portland Japanese Garden from 1968 to 1972. His work includes Anderson Japanese Gardens and Roji-En at the Morikami Museum and Japanese Gardens.

Elizabeth Peters is a trained Garden Guide and the director of Digital Media at BBG, where she oversees the Guides for a Greener Planet imprint and the Garden's website.

Jeanne Rostaing is a frequent contributor to *Gardenista*. She has been a first-round judge for BBG's Greenest Block in Brooklyn contest, and since 2011, she has been the coordinator for Plant-O-Rama, an annual symposium and trade show at BBG.

Douglas M. Roth is the publisher of *Sukiya Living Magazine: The Journal of Japanese Gardening*. He trained as a gardener in Japan and has lived there for much of the past 25 years. Each year he organizes a 13-day garden and walking tour of Kyoto.

Sarah Schmidt is the managing editor of BBG's Guides for a Green Planet imprint. Her previous titles include *Green Roofs and Rooftop Gardens* and the award-winning *Kid's Guide to Exploring Nature*. She also curates the Garden's blog.

ILLUSTRATIONS

Asher Browne 95

Hoichi Kurisu 11

Rick Orlosky 29, 35, 41, 48, 55, 60, 67, 72

PHOTOS

Jeffery Anderson 8, 13

Anderson Japanese Gardens 52

Asticou Azalea Garden 38, 40, 43 (4)

Blanca Begert 44 (bottom)

Bjoernord 17

Asher Browne 74, 77 (2), 78 (right), 82, 86

Louis Buhle 7

Rebecca Bullene 31 (top right),

83, 85 (top left, top right, middle right)

Chicago Botanic Garden 61 (2)

David M. Cobb Cover, 24, 30, 32, 45 (bottom), 46, 49, 50 (4), 51, 54, 56, 57 (all but top left), 58, 64, 70, 73, 87

Cquest 16

Alison Dorfman 31 (top left), 45 (top)

Lindsey Filowitz 63

Fjkelfeimvvn 19

Brian Funk 4, 22 (bottom), 23 (third from top), 88, 94

Bernard Gagnon 23 (top)

Jakub Halun 23 (second from top)

The Huntington 34, 36, 37, 45 (second from top)

Japanesperterna.se 14

Robyn Messner 66 (right)

Dana Miller 31

Morikami Museum and Japanese Gardens 44 (top), 66 (left), 68, 69 (4)

Elizabeth Peters 31 (bottom left), 44 (middle), 85 (bottom right, middle left), 90, 93, 97, 98 (3), 99 (4)

Antonio M. Rosario 26, 28, 45 (third from top)

Sarah Schmidt 31 (middle left), 57 (top left), 78 (left), 80

Steven Severinghaus 2, 85 (bottom left)

Jeremy Thorpe 42

Katsuki Yamanaka 20

Index

Note: Page references in italics indicate illustrations or captions; in bold, glossary terms.

Guides for a Greener Planet

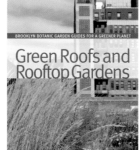

Promoting Organic and Sustainable Gardening

Brooklyn Botanic Garden's award-winning guides provide expert advice in a practical, compact format. To order other fine titles, visit bbg.org/handbooks. Learn more about Brooklyn Botanic Garden at bbg.org.